Standardized Test Prep Handbook

American Civics

HOLT, RINEHART AND WINSTON

A Harcourt Education Company

Austin • Orlando • Chicago • New York • Toronto • London • San Diego

ISBN 0-03-067707-6

6 082 05

Table of Contents

Part 1: Activities

Part 2: Practice Tests

Part 3:

Part 1: Activities

Activity 1 Reading Comprehension: We the People

Directions: Darken the circle for the correct answer, or write your answer in the space provided.

> **TRY THIS** Read each selection and each question twice. Check your answers by looking back in the selection.

Sample A   The Meaning of Civics

> Civics is the study of what it means to be a U.S. citizen—a legally recognized member of the country. The word *civics* comes from the Latin *civis*, meaning "citizen." The concept of citizenship originated in ancient Greece. It was then adopted by the Romans. The Romans used the term to separate people living in the city of Rome from those living in territories that Rome had conquered.

Why are the civilizations of ancient Greece and Rome important to the study of civics?

A because civics was first taught in these societies

B because the ancient Greeks and Romans defined the concept of citizenship

C because "civis" is a Latin term

D because Rome was very powerful

> **THINK IT THROUGH** The correct answer is <u>B</u>. The third and fourth sentences explain that the ancient Greeks originated the concept of citizenship and then the Romans adopted it.

U.S. Immigration Policy

Since its founding, the United States has been settled and populated by people from all over the world. During its early history, the new country provided economic opportunities for immigrants. Agricultural workers and factory laborers were needed as the country grew and the economy expanded. As a result, U.S. policies on immigration allowed unlimited immigration to the United States during the first half of the 1800s.

Because some immigrants were willing to work for lower wages than Americans were, some people wanted to change the immigration policy. During the 1880s the federal government placed some restrictions on immigration. In the 1920s the United States began limiting the number of immigrants who could be admitted to the country each year. The government also established quotas, or set numbers, for how many immigrants could come from a particular country or region.

U.S immigration policy today is guided by the Immigration Act of 1990. Under this law the cap on immigration for 1995 and beyond was set at 675,000 immigrants a year. Preference is given to spouses and children of U.S. citizens, people who have valuable job skills, and permanent resident aliens. Aliens are people in the United States who are citizens of another country. Refugees, or people fleeing persecution in their home countries, are not subject to this annual limit. Instead, the president works with Congress to set different limits for the number of refugees allowed to enter the United States.

SA Ⓐ Ⓑ Ⓒ Ⓓ

1 **This selection is mostly about—**

A why people want to immigrate to the United States.

B the process of immigration.

C the history of U.S. immigration policy.

D the number of immigrants in the United States.

2 **In this selection, the word immigrant means—**

F a citizen of a country.

G a person who comes to another country to live.

H a person who likes to travel.

J a person who has another culture.

3 **Why were there few limitations on immigration before the 1800s?**

A because there were no quotas

B because the president and Congress wanted many immigrants

C because agricultural and factory workers were needed as the country grew

D because life was different then

4 **Why were quotas established?**

F because some people did not like immigrants

G because some immigrants were willing to work for lower wages than some Americans

H because there were not enough jobs

J because people stopped wanting to come to the United States

5 **In this selection, alien means—**

A someone from another planet.

B something that is different.

C a person in the United States who is a citizen of another country.

D anyone who is not a U.S. citizen.

6 **Who determines the number of refugees the United States accepts each year?**

F the citizens of the United States

G the leaders of other countries

H the president and Congress

J the president's cabinet

7 **What are refugees?**

A immigrants from a particular country or region

B immigrants with desirable job skills

C aliens

D people from other countries who are fleeing persecution

8 **Who has special preference for immigration?**

F spouses and children of U.S. citizens

G people who have valuable job skills

H permanent resident aliens

J all of the above

9 **Write a sentence that sums up the main idea of this selection.**

_____

_____

_____

_____

1 (A) (B) (C) (D)　　3 (A) (B) (C) (D)　　5 (A) (B) (C) (D)　　7 (A) (B) (C) (D)　　9 Open-ended

2 (F) (G) (H) (J)　　4 (F) (G) (H) (J)　　6 (F) (G) (H) (J)　　8 (F) (G) (H) (J)

Activity 2 Reading Vocabulary: Foundations of Government

Directions: Darken the circle for the correct answer, or write your answer in the space provided.

| TRY THIS | Read the sentence in the box. Decide what the underlined word means. Then find the word or words with nearly the same meaning. |

Sample A

> Before the American Revolution, many Americans had become underlined accustomed to doing things their own way.

Which word or group of words means the same, or almost the same, as the underlined word in the sample sentence?

A tired of

B afraid of

C used to

D happy with

| THINK IT THROUGH | The correct answer is C. Choice <u>C</u> has nearly the same meaning as the word <u>accustomed</u>. |

---

1 There are about 30 monarchies in the world today. In many of them, the monarch serves as a <u>ceremonial</u> head of state while the power of government lies elsewhere. The word <u>ceremonial</u> means—

A religious service.

B conventional, yet powerless.

C ritual.

D significant.

2 The rulers have <u>absolute</u> control over the people. What does the word <u>absolute</u> mean?

F total

G partial

H no

J little

3 Government provides a <u>means</u> for people to unite and cooperate. Which word defines <u>means</u>?

A value

B place

C way

D reason

4 To safeguard each citizen's liberty, the basic laws of the United States <u>guarantee</u> certain freedoms, such as freedom of speech, freedom of the press, and freedom of religion. To <u>guarantee</u> means—

F to protect.

G to deny.

H to refuse.

J to control.

SA (A) (B) (C) (D)   2 (F) (G) (H) (J)   4 (F) (G) (H) (J)

1 (A) (B) (C) (D)   3 (A) (B) (C) (D)

5 If a government ignores the will of the people, the people have a legitimate right to change the government. Legitimate means—

A obligated.

B dutiful.

C concerned.

D legal.

6 The Declaration of Independence states: "We hold these truths to be self-evident, that all men are created equal, that they are endowed by their Creator with certain unalienable Rights, that among these are Life, Liberty, and the pursuit of Happiness." The word unalienable means—

F cannot be given up or transferred.

G able to deny.

H changeable.

J necessary.

7 The writers of the Articles of Confederation wanted to preserve the states' sovereignty. Sovereignty means—

A power.

B dignity.

C money.

D heritage.

8 Americans suffered difficult times after the Revolutionary War. Trade with Great Britain, which before the war had given American merchants preferential treatment, had slowed. The word preferential means—

F unfair.

G favorable.

H fair.

J neglectful.

9 The most serious disagreement arose over the question of representation in the new national legislature, or lawmaking body. The larger states favored a legislature in which representation would be based on the size of a state's population. The smaller states wanted each state to have an equal number of representatives in the legislature. Summarize this paragraph in your own words.

_____

_____

_____

_____

_____

_____

10 New York City was chosen as the country's temporary capital. What does the word temporary mean?

A permanent

B lasting

C for a limited time

D best

11 Changes in the Articles required the unanimous vote of all 13 states. What does the word unanimous mean?

F united in opinion

G secret

H anonymous

J a negative vote

5 Ⓐ Ⓑ Ⓒ Ⓓ   7 Ⓐ Ⓑ Ⓒ Ⓓ   9 Open-ended   11 Ⓕ Ⓖ Ⓗ Ⓙ
6 Ⓕ Ⓖ Ⓗ Ⓙ   8 Ⓕ Ⓖ Ⓗ Ⓙ   10 Ⓐ Ⓑ Ⓒ Ⓓ

Activity 3 Language: The U.S. Constitution

Directions: Darken the circle for the correct answer, or write your answer in the space provided.

TRY THIS Imagine that you are Anne, the student mentioned below. Use the rules you have learned for writing a rough draft and using correct capitalization, punctuation, word usage, and sentence structure to choose the correct answer.

Sample A Summarizing a Passage

Anne enjoyed reading about the history of the U.S. Constitution. Anne realizes it is necessary to begin organizing the information from the chapter. She plans to write a summary of what she has learned from her reading.

What should Anne do before she starts to write her summary?

A look up the spellings of any unfamiliar words in the section

B make some notes about important points in the passage

C read an article in the local paper about the Constitution

D review rules for punctuation

THINK IT THROUGH The correct answer is <u>B</u>. The first thing Anne should do is make notes about key ideas and details in the passage. It is important to look for main points and supporting details in order to write a clear summary.

Directions: Anne's assignment was to write a report about the U.S. Constitution. A rough draft of the first part of Anne's report is shown on the next page. To answer questions 2–7, read the rough draft carefully. Darken the circle for the correct answer, or write your answer in the space provided.

1   While Anne was writing her summary, she used her dictionary to check how certain nouns are capitalized. Which of the following proper nouns is written correctly?

A mayflower compact
B Mayflower compact
C mayflower Compact
D Mayflower Compact

2   Which sentence in Anne's summary on the next page is a fragment?

F 1
G 2
H 3
J 4

3   Which sentence is missing a comma?

A 4
B 5
C 6
D 7

The Summary of the U.S. Constitution

The ideas in the U.S Constitution's come from the Mayflower
(1)

Compact. The Compact was written when the Pilgrims reached North
(2)

America. In 1620. They wrote the document to create a new government
(3)   (4)

based on the cooperation and consent of the people, a government based

on popular sovereignty is one of the most important ideas in the

Preamble of the Constitution. The constitution set up a federal system
(5)

and state governments. In addition, the framers of the Constitution
(6)

created the legislative branch the executive branch and the judicial

branch. The federal court system of the government. Each branch has
(7)

powers that check, or limit, the powers of the other two branches. I think
(8)

this has all worked out great.

---

4 **Which sentence has incorrect capitalization?**

F   2

G   3

H   4

J   5

5 **Which sentence is not needed in Anne's summary?**

A   5

B   6

C   7

D   8

6 **Which is the topic sentence of the paragraph?**

F   1

G   2

H   3

J   7

7 **Which is a run-on sentence?**

A   3

B   4

C   5

D   6

4 Ⓕ Ⓖ Ⓗ Ⓙ   6 Ⓕ Ⓖ Ⓗ Ⓙ
5 Ⓐ Ⓑ Ⓒ Ⓓ   7 Ⓐ Ⓑ Ⓒ Ⓓ

Activity 4 Social Science: Rights and Responsibilities

Directions: Darken the circle for the correct answer, or write your answer in the space provided.

TRY THIS	Read the sentence in the box. Decide which answer best summarizes the sentence.

Sample A

According to President John F. Kennedy, "The right to vote in a free American election is the most powerful and precious right in the world and it must not be denied on the grounds of race or color."

This statement means—

A President Kennedy urged people to vote for him.

B Certain people should not be allowed to vote in elections.

C America demands that its citizens vote.

D President Kennedy felt that no one should be denied the right to vote.

THINK IT THROUGH	The correct answer is D. Choice <u>D</u> best summarizes the meaning of President Kennedy's words. There is no information in the other sentences to support the answers.

Women in the United States were not the only women who struggled for the right to vote. Nor were they the first to achieve it. This distinction belongs to the women of New Zealand, who fought a long campaign for suffrage.

When a petition of signatures requesting women's suffrage was first sent to the New Zealand Parliament, the members laughed. It was not until suffragist Kate Sheppard presented the legislature with a 300-yard-long petition, signed by almost one fourth of all New Zealand women, that the women were taken seriously.

In 1893 New Zealand became the first self-governing country to grant women suffrage. American women struggling for this right used the New Zealand victory as proof against the widespread notion that women did not really want the vote.

1 What did the women of New Zealand present the legislature with in 1893?

   A a speech

   B a petition

   C a sit-in

   D a demonstration

2 How did American women struggling for the right to vote use the New Zealand victory?

   F The New Zealand women came to the United States.

   G The American women went to New Zealand.

   H The American women used the New Zealand victory as proof against the notion that women did not want the vote.

   J They read a letter to Congress that the New Zealand women wrote.

SA Ⓐ Ⓑ Ⓒ Ⓓ   **2** Ⓕ Ⓖ Ⓗ Ⓙ

1 Ⓐ Ⓑ Ⓒ Ⓓ

President Lincoln wrote, "That on the first day of January, A.D. 1863, all persons held as slaves within any state or designated part of a state, the people whereof shall then be in rebellion against the United States, shall be then, thenceforward, and forever free; and the executive government of the United States, including the military and naval authority thereof, will recognize and maintain the freedom of such persons and will do no act or acts to repress such persons."

3 Rewrite President Lincoln's statement in your own words:

_____

_____

_____

_____

_____

_____

4 Who is President Lincoln saying will be considered to be rebelling against the United States?

   A slave owners

   B slaves

   C soldiers

   D congressmembers

5 What does <u>repress</u> mean in Lincoln's statement?

   F iron again

   G help

   H encourage

   J keep down

6 What was the name of the Proclamation that Lincoln made during the Civil War?

   A Emancipation

   B U.S.

   C Civil War

   D Citizens'

7 Which amendment to the U.S. Constitution officially ended slavery in the United States?

   F Twelfth

   G Thirteenth

   H Fourteenth

   J Fifteenth

8 What were President Lincoln's major accomplishments as a political leader?

_____

_____

_____

_____

9 About how long did it take before African Americans had truly equal voting rights after the Civil War?

   A 10 years

   B 20 years

   C 50 years

   D 100 years

3 Open-ended   **5** Ⓕ Ⓖ Ⓗ Ⓙ   **7** Ⓕ Ⓖ Ⓗ Ⓙ   **9** Ⓐ Ⓑ Ⓒ Ⓓ
4 Ⓐ Ⓑ Ⓒ Ⓓ   **6** Ⓐ Ⓑ Ⓒ Ⓓ   **8** Open-ended

Activity 5 Reading Comprehension: The Legislative Branch

Directions: Darken the circle for the correct answer, or write your answer in the space provided.

The legislative branch of the federal government makes the country's laws. "Members of Congress are the human connection between the citizen and . . . government," noted one member of Congress. The framers discussed the legislative branch in Article I of the U.S. Constitution to emphasize that representatives of the people would govern the United States.

Congress is the lawmaking body of the federal government. The Constitution states that the Congress shall be composed of two houses—the Senate and the House of Representatives. The leaders who drew up the U.S. Constitution in 1787 created this bicameral legislature for two reasons. First, they established two houses to settle a dispute between the delegates from the large states and those from the small states. The delegates from the small states feared that their states would be dominated by the larger ones. The dispute was settled by the Great Compromise. This compromise provided that each state

would be represented equally in the Senate and according to the size of its population in the House of Representatives. The second reason for having two houses was so that they would serve to check and balance each other within the legislative branch. Having two houses share the responsibility of making the country's laws allows each house to check the actions of the other. As a result, there is less danger that Congress will pass laws in haste or pass laws that are not needed or wanted by the people.

According to the Constitution, the number of representatives each state can elect to the House is based on the size of that state's population. Originally, each state elected one representative for every 30,000 people living in the state. In the first Congress, the Constitution allowed 65 representatives in the House. In 1911 Congress limited the size of the House to 435 members. When Alaska and Hawaii became states, the number was temporarily increased to 437.

---

1 **This selection is mostly about—**

   A the executive branch of government.

   B the Great Compromise.

   C the legislative branch of government.

   D the president.

2 **What is the main role of the legislative branch?**

   F to balance presidential power

   G to make laws for the country

   H to make compromises

   J to help people

3 **Why did the framers of the Constitution design a bicameral legislature?**

   A to protect the smaller states

   B to help settle a disagreement

   C to provide checks and balances for the two houses

   D all of the above

4 **In this selection, the word delegates means—**

   F representatives of the people.

   G a group of politicians.

   H authority figures.

   J lawyers.

---

1 Ⓐ Ⓑ Ⓒ Ⓓ   3 Ⓐ Ⓑ Ⓒ Ⓓ

2 Ⓕ Ⓖ Ⓗ Ⓙ   4 Ⓕ Ⓖ Ⓗ Ⓙ

5 In this selection, the term <u>in haste</u> means—

A not legal.
B in a hurry.
C too slowly.
D without agreement.

6 What is the number of members of the House based upon?

F the size of the state
G the importance of the state
H the amount of money the state generates
J the population of the state

7 Why did Congress change the number of representatives?

A Its members thought that with more members they would be more effective.
B Its members wanted more power.
C Two additional states were added to the Union.
D It would save money.

8 Why do you think that the number of members in the House of Representatives needs to be an odd number?

_____

_____

_____

_____

9 Why are the laws of a country important to its people?

_____

_____

_____

_____

10 What does the word <u>compromise</u> mean?

F to give in
G to lose
H to give up
J to make a settlement in which each side gives up some demands

11 Which Article of the Constitution addresses the legislative branch of the government?

A Article III
B Article II
C Article IV
D Article I

12 In your own words, summarize the important points of this selection.

_____

_____

_____

_____

_____

_____

_____

_____

_____

_____

_____

_____

_____

5 Ⓐ Ⓑ Ⓒ Ⓓ   7 Ⓐ Ⓑ Ⓒ Ⓓ   9 Open-ended   11 Ⓐ Ⓑ Ⓒ Ⓓ
6 Ⓕ Ⓖ Ⓗ Ⓙ   8 Open-ended   10 Ⓕ Ⓖ Ⓗ Ⓙ   12 Open-ended

NAME _____ CLASS _____ DATE _____

Activity 6 Vocabulary: The Executive Branch

Directions: Darken the circle for the correct answer, or write your answer in the space provided.

1 On Inauguration Day, the president-elect swears to "faithfully execute the office of the President of the United States." In this sentence, <u>execute</u> means to—

   A put an end to.
   B buy furniture for.
   C perform.
   D put to death.

2 In his inaugural address, President John F. Kennedy said, "Let the word go forth from this time and place, to friend and foe alike, that the torch has been passed to a new generation of Americans—born in this century, <u>tempered</u> by war, disciplined by a hard and bitter peace, proud of our ancient heritage." What does the word <u>tempered</u> mean?

   F made angry
   G created
   H hurt
   J made stronger

3 <u>Succession</u> means—

   A earlier.
   B coming after.
   C giving away.
   D helping.

4 A presidential <u>reprieve</u> is a—

   F reprimand.
   G postponed punishment.
   H renewed punishment.
   J punishment taken away.

5 A president who is <u>diplomatic</u>—

   A is hard to get along with.
   B gets along well with others.
   C has a lot of diplomas.
   D is difficult to please.

6 Someone who is <u>impartial</u> is—

   F unfair.
   G opinionated.
   H easy to convince.
   J without prejudice.

7 A <u>nominee</u> is—

   A the winner.
   B the loser.
   C a person chosen to run for office.
   D a judge.

8 Although he did not want to be president, George Washington <u>rendered</u> his services to his country. To <u>render</u> means to—

   F surrender.
   G give.
   H refuse.
   J remove.

9 President Washington <u>presided</u> over many key moments in the establishment of the federal government. To <u>preside</u> means to—

   A guide or control.
   B form an opinion.
   C create.
   D present.

1 Ⓐ Ⓑ Ⓒ Ⓓ   3 Ⓐ Ⓑ Ⓒ Ⓓ   5 Ⓐ Ⓑ Ⓒ Ⓓ   7 Ⓐ Ⓑ Ⓒ Ⓓ   9 Ⓐ Ⓑ Ⓒ Ⓓ

2 Ⓕ Ⓖ Ⓗ Ⓙ   4 Ⓕ Ⓖ Ⓗ Ⓙ   6 Ⓕ Ⓖ Ⓗ Ⓙ   8 Ⓕ Ⓖ Ⓗ Ⓙ

10 What is the meaning of the word precedent?

_____

_____

_____

_____

11 What is a consul?

F a counselor

G a U.S. representative abroad

H a group of people

J a congressmember

12 What are regulations?

A facts

B rumors

C warnings

D rules

13 The word provision means something that is—

F supplied for the future.

G denied for the future.

H banned in the future.

J allowed in the future.

14 President George W. Bush addressed Congress and the country with these words: "We will rally the world to this cause by our efforts, by our courage. We will not tire, we will not falter, and we will not fail." What does the verb rally mean?

A to convince

B to tell

C to bring together

D to ask

15 In your own words, describe what a presidential pardon is.

_____

_____

_____

_____

_____

_____

10 Open-ended **12** Ⓐ Ⓑ Ⓒ Ⓓ **14** Ⓐ Ⓑ Ⓒ Ⓓ
11 Ⓕ Ⓖ Ⓗ Ⓙ **13** Ⓕ Ⓖ Ⓗ Ⓙ **15** Open-ended

Activity 7 Language: The Judicial Branch

Directions: Anthony was asked to write a brief biography of Thurgood Marshall. Here is his rough draft of the first part of the biography. Read the rough draft carefully. Darken the circle for the correct answer, or write your answer in the space provided.

The Life of Thurgood Marshall

Thurgood Marshall, the first african american justice serving on the
(1)

Supreme Court, was born in Maryland in 1908. After graduating from
          (2)

Howard Law School in 1933, he became legal counsel for the National

Association for the Advancement of Colored People (naacp). Marshall
          (3)

helped develop a long-term strategy for abolishing segregation in

schools. In 1954, Marshals most famous victory as legal counsel took place.
   (4)

He won in the Supreme Court case *Brown* v. *Board of Education* which
(5)

outlawed segregation in U.S. public schools.

    In 1961, Marshall was appointed as a federal Court of Appeals judge.
   (6)

He became the first African American justice on the Supreme Court in
(7)

1967 and served for more than 20 years. Known for his commitment to
          (8)

education and justice. In one of Marshall's cases, he accused the majority
     (9)

of "insupportable acquiescence in a system which deprives children in

their earliest years of the chance to reach their full potential as citizens.

Marshall retired from the court in 1991 and died in 1993 at 84 I think that
(10)   **(11)**

Thurgood Marshall was a great man.

---

1   In sentence 1, how should african american be written?

_____

2   Which sentence contains incorrect capitalization of an acronym?

    A   1
    B   2
    C   3
    D   4

3   Which sentence is missing an apostrophe?

    F   4
    G   5
    H   6
    J   7

4   Which sentence is a fragment?

    A   8
    B   9
    C   10
    D   11

5   Write a sentence that summarizes an important accomplishment in Thurgood Marshall's career.

_____

_____

_____

_____

_____

_____

_____

6   Which sentence has an incorrect use of quotation marks?

    F   7
    G   8
    H   9
    J   10

7   In sentence 9, what does the word acquiescence mean?

    A   going along with
    B   arguing against
    C   bitterness
    D   refusing of

8   In your own words, explain Marshall's quote in sentence 9.

_____

_____

_____

_____

9   Which sentence is not needed?

    F   1
    G   5
    H   7
    J   11

10   Which sentence is missing a period?

    A   8
    B   9
    C   10
    D   11

Copyright © by Holt, Rinehart and Winston. All rights reserved.

14

1 Open-ended   3 Ⓕ Ⓖ Ⓗ Ⓙ   5 Open-ended   7 Ⓐ Ⓑ Ⓒ Ⓓ   9 Ⓕ Ⓖ Ⓗ Ⓙ
2 Ⓐ Ⓑ Ⓒ Ⓓ   4 Ⓐ Ⓑ Ⓒ Ⓓ   6 Ⓕ Ⓖ Ⓗ Ⓙ   8 Open-ended   10 Ⓐ Ⓑ Ⓒ Ⓓ

Activity 8 Social Science: State Government

Directions: Darken the circle for the correct answer, or write your answer in the space provided.

1 **What was the purpose of the Tenth Amendment?**

   A to protect the right to vote

   B to protect states' rights

   C to protect the rights of children

   D to protect the federal government

2 **Which is a function of state government?**

   F to establish and maintain schools

   G to conduct elections

   H to regulate business within state borders

   J all of the above

3 **What was the Northwest Ordinance?**

   A a law providing a way for territories to join the United States

   B a group of laws specifically for the northwest states

   C a law prohibiting slavery

   D a law permitting women to vote

4 **What does the "Full Faith and Credit Clause" ensure?**

   F that each state will accept the decisions of courts in other states

   G that each state will grant credit to its citizens

   H that each state will allow citizens to practice their own religion

   J none of the above

5 **Nebraska has a unicameral legislature. What does the word unicameral mean?**

   A one house

   B two houses

   C a combined house

   D no house

6 **What is an _initiative_?**

   F a method of referring questions to the people for a vote

   G a required number of voters who sign a petition

   H a process to begin new legislation

   J all of the above

7 **How is the governor chosen for each state?**

   A He or she is appointed by the president.

   B He or she is appointed by the senators of the state.

   C He or she is elected by a statewide vote.

   D He or she is voted in by Congress.

8 **In a civil case, the person or company filing the complaint, or lawsuit, is referred to as a—**

   F justice of the peace.

   G plaintiff.

   H prosecuting attorney.

   J juror.

1 (A) (B) (C) (D) 3 (A) (B) (C) (D) 5 (A) (B) (C) (D) 7 (A) (B) (C) (D)
2 (F) (G) (H) (J) 4 (F) (G) (H) (J) 6 (F) (G) (H) (J) 8 (F) (G) (H) (J)

9 If you thought that your case was not handled fairly in a trial court, you could—

    A take the case to an appeals court.

    B ask the president to override the decision.

    C sue the judge.

    D picket the courthouse.

10 Governor Michael F. Easley of North Carolina said to his constituents in his inaugural address, "I thank you personally for putting people first and putting party differences aside. Good government is not about Democrats and Republicans. It is about children, seniors, and working families. You put them first. . . . Any state can make progress in good times. It's the great states that make progress in the tough times. It's the darkest hours that draw out our brightest stars."

Rewrite Governor Easley's statement in your own words.

_____

_____

_____

_____

_____

11 What is one of the conditions that must be met in order for people in the United States to serve as lawmakers?

    F They must have a college degree.

    G They must own property.

    H They must have a driver's license.

    J They must be U.S. citizens.

12 How can citizens take direct action in legislation and state government?

    A by creating and signing petitions

    B by voting

    C by running for office

    D all of the above

13 What is one duty of the governor?

    F to propose and veto legislation

    G to advise the president

    H to create jobs for the state

    J to create public school curricula

14 Who helps the governor run the state?

    A the secretary of state

    B the attorney general

    C the state treasurer

    D all of the above

15 In your own words, explain how the appeals process works.

_____

_____

_____

_____

_____

_____

_____

_____

_____

_____

    9 Ⓐ Ⓑ Ⓒ Ⓓ   **11** Ⓕ Ⓖ Ⓗ Ⓙ   **13** Ⓕ Ⓖ Ⓗ Ⓙ   **15** Open-ended

    10 Open-ended   **12** Ⓐ Ⓑ Ⓒ Ⓓ   **14** Ⓐ Ⓑ Ⓒ Ⓓ

Activity 9 Reading Comprehension: Local Government

Directions: Darken the circle for the correct answer, or write your answer in the space provided.

The town form of government began in the New England colonies. Each colony received a grant of land from the king of England. The colonists established small towns, where they built their homes and churches. At the edges of the towns, the settlers established their farms. Each day they left their homes and worked on the farms. The colonists considered these outlying farms to be part of their towns. Later some of the settlers moved to the farms. As long as these farms were located within the town limits, people living on them were considered residents of that town. As a result, New England towns stretched out into the countryside.

In some areas, the settlers set up a village form of government. Only the village itself, which included the homes of the settlers and other buildings, was overseen by the village government. The outlying parts of the settlement were not considered part of the village. These areas later came under the rule of the county government.

As other people pushed farther west, they established new settlements. Some of them called their settlements boroughs. Thus, many different names were used for these small settlements.

The people of the early New England towns created a simple yet effective form of local government—the town meeting. Town residents and people from surrounding farms met regularly in the town hall. At these public meetings, citizens discussed issues and problems and decided how they should be handled.

Citizens had the opportunity to speak on any issue. After all opinions were heard, the people at the meeting voted on the issue. In this way, each citizen had a direct vote in the government. A New England town meeting was direct democracy in action. Some small New England towns still manage their business in this manner. Town meetings are also held in several states in the Midwest.

1 **This selection is mostly about—**

   A   the early settlers of this nation.

   B   the development of early town government.

   C   the importance of voting.

   D   the development of cities.

2 **What did the village include?**

   F   homes

   G   buildings in town

   H   both F and G

   J   none of the above

3 **Why did the settlers have town meetings?**

   A   to vote on issues

   B   to help settle disagreements

   C   to discuss issues

   D   all of the above

4 **In this passage, what does the term** *direct democracy* **mean?**

   F   Representatives were elected to speak for the people.

   G   The democracy was forthright.

   H   Each citizen had a vote.

   J   all of the above

1 Ⓐ Ⓑ Ⓒ Ⓓ   3 Ⓐ Ⓑ Ⓒ Ⓓ
2 Ⓕ Ⓖ Ⓗ Ⓙ   4 Ⓕ Ⓖ Ⓗ Ⓙ

5 **How did the town form of government begin in the New England colonies?**

A   by the hard work of the settlers

B   by the movement of the settlers to farms

C   through the village government

D   through a grant of land from the king of England

6 **Whose rule did the outlying parts of the settlement fall under?**

F   the village

G   the county government

H   the state

J   the mayor

7 **How were the early towns and villages alike?**

A   They both considered outlying areas to be under their rule.

B   They both wanted more power in the hands of the politicians.

C   They were both large governed areas.

D   They were both small governed areas.

8 **Why was it significant that the opinions of all citizens were heard, as opposed to only those of a few representatives?**

_____

_____

_____

_____

_____

9 **In your own words, state the reason why some New England towns and Midwestern towns still use town meetings.**

_____

_____

_____

_____

_____

10 **What would be an appropriate title for the passage?**

F   Life in the Early Settlements

G   The Rule of the King of England

H   The Beginnings of Democracy

J   The Importance of Town Meetings

11 **How were early towns and villages different?**

A   Town governments considered outlying areas to be under their rule, but villages did not.

B   Towns did not allow citizens to vote, but villages did.

C   Villages held town meetings, but towns did not.

D   Towns supported the king of England, but villages did not.

12 **Summarize the main points of this selection.**

_____

_____

_____

_____

5 Ⓐ Ⓑ Ⓒ Ⓓ   7 Ⓐ Ⓑ Ⓒ Ⓓ   9 Open-ended   11 Ⓐ Ⓑ Ⓒ Ⓓ

6 Ⓕ Ⓖ Ⓗ Ⓙ   8 Open-ended   10 Ⓕ Ⓖ Ⓗ Ⓙ   12 Open-ended

Activity 10 Vocabulary: Electing Leaders

Directions: Darken the circle for the correct answer, or write your answer in the space provided.

1 President Washington's warnings about political parties were <u>unheeded</u>. What does the word <u>unheeded</u> mean?

  A not followed

  B unethical

  C not legal

  D followed exactly

2 Democrats, led by Andrew Jackson, <u>championed</u> the cause of common people. The word <u>championed</u> means—

  F fought against.

  G supported.

  H opposed.

  J denied.

3 Governments formed in a two-party system tend to be <u>stable</u>. The word <u>stable</u> means—

  A weak.

  B strong.

  C unethical.

  D overpowering.

4 A <u>coalition</u> is—

  F an agreement between two or more parties to work together.

  G an agreement between two or more parties to work against one another.

  H an agreement between coal miners.

  J none of the above

5 Few third-party candidates have done as well as Theodore Roosevelt and Ross Perot. Among the most <u>notable</u> third-party candidates were George Wallace and John Anderson. <u>Notable</u> means—

  A hard to get along with.

  B most likely to win.

  C most likely to lose.

  D worthy of notice.

6 <u>Totalitarian</u> governments usually have only one party. <u>Totalitarian</u> means—

  F the government is weak.

  G the people have total control.

  H control is shared.

  J one party has complete control.

7 The Democratic and Republican Parties have different platforms. What is a <u>party platform</u>?

  A a proposed program for the country

  B a written statement of views

  C a raised stage for speeches

  D both A and B

8 The <u>informed</u> voter has studied hard to identify the candidate whose views most closely resemble his or her own. <u>Informed</u> means—

  F knowledgeable.

  G ignorant.

  H supportive.

  J patriotic.

1 Ⓐ Ⓑ Ⓒ Ⓓ   3 Ⓐ Ⓑ Ⓒ Ⓓ   5 Ⓐ Ⓑ Ⓒ Ⓓ   7 Ⓐ Ⓑ Ⓒ Ⓓ
2 Ⓕ Ⓖ Ⓗ Ⓙ   4 Ⓕ Ⓖ Ⓗ Ⓙ   6 Ⓕ Ⓖ Ⓗ Ⓙ   8 Ⓕ Ⓖ Ⓗ Ⓙ

9 Independent candidates usually receive only <u>grassroots</u> support. What does the word <u>grassroots</u> mean?

A support of poor citizens

B support of undecided citizens

C support of the media

D support from many individuals at the local level

10 In your own words, describe what a two-party system is.

_____

_____

_____

_____

_____

11 A runoff is an election between the two leading vote <u>recipients</u> to determine the winner. <u>Recipients</u> are—

F citizens.

G receivers.

H politicians.

J the losers.

12 There are many <u>nonpartisan</u> organizations like the League of Women Voters that provide information about national and local elections. <u>Nonpartisan</u> means

A committed to the Republican Party.

B not connected to either political party.

C supportive of the Democratic Party.

D none of the above

13 Political parties affect every one of us. Political parties are interested in <u>practical</u> politics. The word <u>practical</u> means—

F essential.

G unessential.

H frivolous.

J all of the above

14 In your own words, describe political parties and their functions.

_____

_____

_____

_____

_____

15 Describe the difference between a <u>primary</u> and a <u>general</u> election.

_____

_____

_____

_____

_____

_____

16 In presidential elections, the <u>popular</u> vote is—

A the votes American citizens cast.

B the votes electors cast.

C the votes senators cast.

D the majority of votes cast.

9 Ⓐ Ⓑ Ⓒ Ⓓ 11 Ⓕ Ⓖ Ⓗ Ⓙ 13 Ⓕ Ⓖ Ⓗ Ⓙ 15 Open-ended
10 Open-ended 12 Ⓐ Ⓑ Ⓒ Ⓓ 14 Open-ended 16 Ⓐ Ⓑ Ⓒ Ⓓ

Activity 11 Language: The Political System

Directions: Paul was asked to write a brief paper on the importance of interest groups to the U.S. government. Here is the rough draft of his paper. Read the rough draft carefully. Darken the circle for the correct answer, or write your answer in the space provided.

Many Americans join interest groups. These groups are people with a common interest
(1)   **(2)**

who try to influence the policies of the government Interest groups are not the same
                                  (3)

thing as political parties. Interest groups sometimes support particular candidates, but
                (4)

their main interest is in influencing public policies that affect their members. Interest
                                  (5)

groups have existed throughout our history. People who favored the Constitution
                         (6)

fought to support it, people opposed to slavery formed groups to fight against it.

      there are lots of different kinds of interest groups. For businesses, farms, older
(7)   **(8)**

citizens, teachers, veterans. Each group represents interests of its members; Some of
                (9)   **(10)**

these include the united mine workers of america, american farm bureau, national

association of manufacturers. Some interests groups promote justice and equality for
                (11)

their members; for example, the NAACP promotes racial equality and NOW protects

womens rights. Other groups called public interest groups promote interests of the
                (12)

general public rather than just one part of it they help all of us.

      Interests groups vary in size, goals, and budgets. Most interest groups use similar
(13)   **(14)**

methods to write the president or senators or representatives about certain bills.

Lobbyists represent the interest groups. Lobbyists are paid for their work by the interest
(15)   **(16)**

groups. I would like to be a lobbyist when I graduate from college.
      (17)

1 Which sentence is a comma splice?

   A 4

   B 5

   C 6

   D 7

2 What is missing in sentence 2?

   F a capital letter

   G a period

   H a quotation mark

   J a verb

3 Which sentence needs an apostrophe?

   A 8

   B 9

   C 10

   D 11

4 Where is the sentence fragment in the paper?

   F 7

   G 8

   H 9

   J 10

5 In sentence 10, what is incorrect?

   A misplaced commas

   B punctuation

   C capitalization

   D subject/verb agreement

6 Create an appropriate title for Paul's essay in the space provided.

_____

7 Combine sentences 15 and 16 into one sentence that is correctly punctuated.

_____

_____

8 Why do you think interest groups are important?

_____

_____

_____

_____

_____

9 Which sentence is not needed?

   F 14

   G 15

   H 16

   J 17

10 Which sentence is a run-on sentence?

   A 11

   B 12

   C 13

   D 14

11 Which of the following is the best topic sentence for paragraph 2?

   F There are too many interest groups.

   G There is a good deal of prejudice against people in the United States so we need interest groups.

   H There are several different types of interest groups in the United States.

   J Interest groups are not needed.

1 Ⓐ Ⓑ Ⓒ Ⓓ   **3** Ⓐ Ⓑ Ⓒ Ⓓ   **5** Ⓐ Ⓑ Ⓒ Ⓓ   **7** Open-ended   **9** Ⓕ Ⓖ Ⓗ Ⓙ   **11** Ⓕ Ⓖ Ⓗ Ⓙ

2 Ⓕ Ⓖ Ⓗ Ⓙ   **4** Ⓕ Ⓖ Ⓗ Ⓙ   **6** Open-ended   **8** Open-ended   **10** Ⓐ Ⓑ Ⓒ Ⓓ

Activity 12 Social Science: Paying for Government

Directions: Darken the circle for the correct answer, or write your answer in the space provided.

1   **What is the national debt?**

   A debt that citizens owe to the government

   B debt that politicians have created

   C debt that the states owe

   D money that the government has borrowed

2   **What is the income tax rate based upon?**

   F the amount of money the government needs for the year

   G the amount of national debt

   H the amount a citizen earns in a year

   J the rate of inflation

3   **What does equal application mean?**

   A Every citizen must be treated fairly.

   B Taxes are applied at the same rate for similar items.

   C Taxes are not applied at an equal rate.

   D none of the above

4   **What are tax exemptions?**

   F people who do not have to pay taxes

   G taxes that are not required by law

   H the money a citizen receives from the government

   J money that taxpayers are allowed to deduct, or subtract, for themselves and each dependent

5   **What is a tariff?**

   A taxes the U.S. government collects on products imported from foreign countries

   B taxes U.S. government pays on products exported to foreign countries

   C a process to begin new legislation

   D all of the above

6   **A surplus occurs when—**

   F a government borrows money to create revenue.

   G a government lends money to other countries

   H a government does not collect as much money as it spends.

   J a government collects more money than it spends.

7   **A deficit is—**

   A a defect.

   B a shortage of money.

   C a bill.

   D a lie.

8   **Who proposes the national budget?**

   F the Speaker of the House

   G the Senate

   H the Supreme Court

   J the executive branch

1 Ⓐ Ⓑ Ⓒ Ⓓ   3 Ⓐ Ⓑ Ⓒ Ⓓ   5 Ⓐ Ⓑ Ⓒ Ⓓ   7 Ⓐ Ⓑ Ⓒ Ⓓ
2 Ⓕ Ⓖ Ⓗ Ⓙ   4 Ⓕ Ⓖ Ⓗ Ⓙ   6 Ⓕ Ⓖ Ⓗ Ⓙ   8 Ⓕ Ⓖ Ⓗ Ⓙ

9 In your own words, define *property tax.*

_____

_____

_____

_____

_____

_____

_____

10 A balanced budget is achieved when—

A taxpayers' money is distributed equally.

B revenue equals expenditures.

C expenditures are greater than revenue.

D revenues are greater than expenditures.

11 What is a progressive tax?

F a tax exemption

G a tax for progressive ideas

H a tax for progress

J a tax that takes a larger percentage of income from high-income groups than from low-income groups

12 What sorts of things are considered personal property?

A stocks and bonds

B jewelry

C cars and boats

D all of the above

13 Which branch of government turns the budget into law?

F the executive branch

G the judicial branch

H the legislative branch

J all of the above

14 Summarize how the government goes about collecting taxes to pay for its work.

_____

_____

_____

_____

_____

_____

_____

15 What is a government bond?

A a certificate stating that the government has borrowed a sum of money from the owner of the bond

B a certificate stating that a person owes the government a certain sum

C a certificate stating that one government owes money to another government

D none of the above

9 Open-ended   11 (F) (G) (H) (J)   13 (F) (G) (H) (J)   15 (A) (B) (C) (D)
10 (A) (B) (C) (D)   12 (A) (B) (C) (D)   14 Open-ended

NAME _____ CLASS _____ DATE _____

Activity 13 Reading Comprehension: Citizenship and the Family

Directions: Darken the circle for the correct answer, or write your answer in the space provided.

Life on early American farms was difficult. There was little time for play or schooling. Some farm children attended a one-room schoolhouse. However, many children received a basic education at home.

The early farm family was the basic work unit in the colonies. Families themselves produced most of what they needed to survive. The family depended on all of its members to do their part. As children got older and married, they did not always move away from home. Often they brought their wives or husbands with them to live on the family farm.

In these large families, everyone lived and worked together. As a man grew older, he took on lighter chores while his son or son-in-law did the heavier work. As a woman grew older, she spent less time on heavy household chores. She spent more time sewing or looking after her grandchildren. Young or old, family members contributed what they could and received the care they needed. The need to work together developed a strong spirit of cooperation.

During the 1800s American life began to change rapidly. One hundred years ago, six of every ten Americans lived on farms or in rural areas. Today only one in four Americans lives in a rural area. This change came about because of the remarkable progress in science and technology during the 1800s.

New inventions and improved methods of production led to the rise of factories. These factories used new technology and work methods to produce large quantities of goods. In turn, the growth of factories encouraged the growth of cities, as people moved to urban areas seeking factory jobs. At the same time, fewer people were needed to work on the farms because of improvements in farm machinery and equipment. This movement of Americans from the farms to the cities resulted in vast changes in family life.

Life in the cities was much different for families than farm life had been. For example, families could no longer spend as much time together. Fathers now worked long hours outside the home to earn money. Until national child-labor laws were passed in the 1930s, many children worked in factories to earn money for the family.

1 **This selection is mostly about—**

A the emergence of factories.

B the changing American family.

C the roles of family members.

D the development of farm equipment.

2 **Which of the following helped to drastically change the family unit?**

F science and technology

G families moving into rural areas

H children moving away from home

J failed crops

3 **Why did grown children not move away from home during the early days of American history?**

A There were not enough houses to live in.

B There was not enough land on which to build houses.

C The farm required many people to work it.

D They wanted their parents to watch the small children while the adult children worked in the factories.

1 Ⓐ Ⓑ Ⓒ Ⓓ   **3** Ⓐ Ⓑ Ⓒ Ⓓ   25
2 Ⓕ Ⓖ Ⓗ Ⓙ

4 Who was largely responsible for the education and religious training of children in the colonial family?

    F the community

    G the church

    H the family

    J the local school board

5 When were the national child-labor laws passed?

    A in the 1730s

    B in the 1830s

    C in the 1930s

    D none of the above

6 How many Americans live in rural areas today?

    F 6 out of 10

    G 4 out of 10

    H 2 out of 4

    J 1 out of 4

7 Why did families move to the city?

    A They thought there would be more to do.

    B They came to work in the factories.

    C Life was easier.

    D There were not enough farms.

8 In your own words, describe what happened to the family unit when families moved to the city.

_____

_____

_____

_____

9 When did the American family experience rapid change?

    F during the 1600s

    G during the 1700s

    H during the 1800s

    J during the 1900s

10 What is one major difference between the colonial family and the present-day American family?

    A The colonial family did not stay in one unit.

    B The colonial family did not spend time together.

    C The colonial family tended to be a self-sufficient unit.

    D The colonial family moved around the country.

11 In your own words, summarize what you think daily life was like for early farm families.

_____

_____

_____

_____

_____

4 Ⓕ Ⓖ Ⓗ Ⓙ   **6** Ⓕ Ⓖ Ⓗ Ⓙ   **8** Open-ended **10** Ⓐ Ⓑ Ⓒ Ⓓ
5 Ⓐ Ⓑ Ⓒ Ⓓ   **7** Ⓐ Ⓑ Ⓒ Ⓓ   **9** Ⓕ Ⓖ Ⓗ Ⓙ **11** Open-ended

NAME_____ CLASS_____ DATE_____

Activity 14 Vocabulary: Citizenship in School

Directions: Darken the circle for the correct answer, or write your answer in the space provided.

1 **What is critical thinking?**

  A criticizing others

  B thinking we do to reach solutions and solve problems

  C thinking creatively

  D thinking like others

2 **An answer you get through insight—**

  F suddenly springs to mind.

  G seems to come out of nowhere.

  H happens after you study the problem and rule out other answers.

  J all of the above

3 **When people are conditioned, they—**

  A expect to be rewarded or punished according to their behavior.

  B are easily persuaded to do something.

  C do not expect to be rewarded or punished according to their behavior.

  D none of the above

4 **School attendance is compulsory for young people through age 16. Compulsory means—**

  F optional.

  G excellent.

  H average.

  J mandatory.

5 **Thomas Jefferson thought that in order for a democracy to operate effectively, its citizens had to be educated. What does the word effectively mean?**

  A producing a positive result

  B producing a negative result

  C producing a lasting result

  D producing an interesting result

6 **The law in 1647 provided for every town of 50 families or more to hire a schoolteacher. By doing so, Massachusetts shifted the responsibility for schooling from the home to the community. In this passage, shifted means—**

  F lifted.

  G moved.

  H replaced.

  J refused.

7 **The Declaration of Independence states "that all men are created equal, that they are endowed by their Creator with certain unalienable rights, that among these are life, liberty, and the pursuit of happiness." In this passage, the word endowed means—**

  A refused.

  B prevented.

  C allowed.

  D given.

8 In the past, students with special needs were <u>isolated</u>. <u>Isolated</u> means—

    F included with the group.

    G separated.

    H ignored.

    J encouraged.

9 The U.S. Supreme Court has held that no school-<u>sponsored</u> prayer or Bible reading shall be allowed during the school day. <u>Sponsored</u> in this passage means—

    A funded.

    B proposed.

    C supported.

    D required.

10 In your own words, describe why it is important to a democracy to have educated citizens.

_____

_____

_____

_____

_____

11 Schools should be places where young people can grow in mind, body, and spirit. Sports, clubs, social events, and creative arts are a part of each person's education. They are called—

    F core classes.

    G unnecessary classes.

    H extracurricular activities.

    J nonessential classes.

12 Another challenge facing the educational system is the need for educational <u>reform</u>. <u>Reform</u> means—

    A change.

    B punishment.

    C excellence.

    D none of the above

13 Public education costs American taxpayers around $326 billion a year, including <u>expenditures</u> by the federal government of about $22 billion. What does the word <u>expenditures</u> mean in this sentence?

    F taxes.

    G investments.

    H profits.

    J spending.

14 In your own words, describe some of the options that are available to the American student for education after high school.

_____

_____

_____

_____

15 Describe the difference between undergraduate and graduate school.

_____

_____

_____

_____

8 Ⓕ Ⓖ Ⓗ Ⓙ   **10** Open-ended   **12** Ⓐ Ⓑ Ⓒ Ⓓ   **14** Open-ended

9 Ⓐ Ⓑ Ⓒ Ⓓ   **11** Ⓕ Ⓖ Ⓗ Ⓙ   **13** Ⓕ Ⓖ Ⓗ Ⓙ   **15** Open-ended

Activity 15 Language: Citizenship in the Community

Directions: Libby was asked to write a brief paper on the importance of volunteerism in the community. Here is her rough draft of the paper. Read the rough draft carefully. Darken the circle for the correct answer, or write your answer in the space provided.

Communities around the country rely on volunteers to help the sick,
(1)

poor, elderly and disabled. Schools, park systems political organizations
(2)

and hospitals benefit from the countless hours that Americans give to

these institutions every year Volunteering are one of the most patriotic
(3)

things an American can do for his or her country. Historically, volunteers
(4)

have helped in some of the greatest national tragedies our country has

faced. During World War I and II, Americans around the country made
(5)

bandages, collected materials for the war effort, and worked in hospitals

serving the injured. During the September 11, 2001, tragedy, Americans
(6)

from all over pitched in to help the families of the victims. Some
(7)

communities have volunteer groups. Some are small while others are
(8)

large national organizations. Some volunteers may be called upon to
(9)

solve a specific problem, like cleaning up a park, or play ground. Which
(10)

is great. Some schools require that their students volunteer for a certain
(11)

number of hours a week.

america could not be such a strong country without its volunteers.
(12)

There a significant part of every community. Go volunteer!
(13)   **(14)**

1   Which two forms of punctuation is
    sentence 2 missing?

    A   semicolon and period
    B   capitalization and comma
    C   comma and period
    D   question mark and comma

2   What is sentence 12 missing?

    F   a capital letter
    G   a period
    H   a quotation mark
    J   a verb

3   Which sentence has a subject/verb
    agreement error?

    A   1
    B   2
    C   3
    D   4

4   Where is the sentence fragment in
    the paper?

    F   9
    G   10
    H   11
    J   12

5   Where in the first paragraph should
    there be a new paragraph break?

    A   before sentence 5
    B   before sentence 6
    C   before sentence 7
    D   before sentence 8

6   Create an appropriate title for
    Libby's essay in the space provided.

    _____

    _____

7   Combine sentences 8 and 9 into one
    sentence that is correctly punctuated.

    _____

    _____

    _____

8   Write in your own words why
    volunteering is important to the
    United States.

    _____

    _____

    _____

    _____

    _____

    _____

9   How could sentences 7, 8, and 9 be
    improved?
    F   correct punctuation
    G   vary sentence beginnings
    H   correct capitalization
    J   none of the above

10 In Sentence 13, "There" should be
    written as—

    A   Their
    B   They are
    C   The
    D   A

11 Which sentence is not necessary?

    F   11
    G   12
    H   13
    J   14

Copyright © by Holt, Rinehart and Winston. All rights reserved.

1 Ⓐ Ⓑ Ⓒ Ⓓ   3 Ⓐ Ⓑ Ⓒ Ⓓ   5 Ⓐ Ⓑ Ⓒ Ⓓ   7 Open-ended   9 Ⓕ Ⓖ Ⓗ Ⓙ   11 Ⓕ Ⓖ Ⓗ Ⓙ
2 Ⓕ Ⓖ Ⓗ Ⓙ   4 Ⓕ Ⓖ Ⓗ Ⓙ   6 Open-ended   8 Open-ended   10 Ⓐ Ⓑ Ⓒ Ⓓ

NAME _____ CLASS _____ DATE _____

Activity 16 Social Science: Citizenship and the Law

Directions: Darken the circle for the correct answer, or write your answer in the space provided.

1 **How are crimes classified?**

   A by the number of crimes a criminal has committed

   B by the severity of the crime

   C by the police officer

   D by the community

2 **What is fraud?**

   F felonies

   G homicide

   H victimless crimes

   J taking someone else's money or property through dishonesty

3 **What is larceny?**

   A the theft of property without the use of force or violence

   B the theft of property with the use of violence

   C kidnapping

   D rape

4 **When someone is acquitted of a crime, he or she is—**

   F convicted of the crime.

   G found not guilty.

   H punished for the crime.

   J held responsible for the crime.

5 **In a court of law, a sentence is—**

   A a subject and a verb.

   B the judge's decision on punishment for the crime.

   C the defendant's decision on punishment for the crime.

   D the prosecutor's decision on punishment for the crime.

6 **For minor offenses, the judge may agree to release the suspect on his or her own recognizance. What does own recognizance mean?**

   F innocence

   G with bail

   H without having to post bail

   J admission of guilt

7 **An indictment is—**

   A an arrest.

   B a conviction.

   C a formal charge.

   D a pardon.

8 **The Bill of Rights states that before any arrest can be made, the officer must have—**

   F probable cause.

   G a warrant.

   H some evidence.

   J all of the above

Copyright © by Holt, Rinehart and Winston. All rights reserved.

1 Ⓐ Ⓑ Ⓒ Ⓓ   **3** Ⓐ Ⓑ Ⓒ Ⓓ   **5** Ⓐ Ⓑ Ⓒ Ⓓ   **7** Ⓐ Ⓑ Ⓒ Ⓓ

2 Ⓕ Ⓖ Ⓗ Ⓙ   **4** Ⓕ Ⓖ Ⓗ Ⓙ   **6** Ⓕ Ⓖ Ⓗ Ⓙ   **8** Ⓕ Ⓖ Ⓗ Ⓙ

9   After serving a part of their sentences, prisoners are eligible for parole. What is parole?

   A   early release
   B   another trial
   C   rehabilitation
   D   a new lawyer

10   In your own words, describe the concepts of imprisonment as punishment and rehabilitation.

   _____

   _____

   _____

   _____

   _____

   _____

   _____

11   How do most states define juvenile?

   F   a person under the age of 15
   G   a person under the age of 21
   H   a person under the age of 10
   J   a person under the age of 18

12   What is probation?

   A   a police officer asking a suspect questions
   B   an investigation of a crime
   C   a period of time during which offenders are given an opportunity to show that they can reform
   D   none of the above

13   What are some of the possible reasons that people commit crimes?

   F   poverty
   G   dropping out of school
   H   alcohol and drugs
   J   all of the above

14   In your own words, write a brief summary of how the justice system goes about convicting a person of a crime, or declaring their innocence of the crime.

   _____

   _____

   _____

   _____

   _____

   _____

   _____

   _____

9 Ⓐ Ⓑ Ⓒ Ⓓ   11 Ⓕ Ⓖ Ⓗ Ⓙ   13 Ⓕ Ⓖ Ⓗ Ⓙ
10 Open-ended   12 Ⓐ Ⓑ Ⓒ Ⓓ   14 Open-ended

Activity 17 Reading Comprehension: The Economic System

Directions: Darken the circle for the correct answer, or write your answer in the space provided.

Americans enjoy important economic freedoms. Because of these freedoms, the U.S. economic system is often called a free-market economy, or simply a market economy. Our economic freedoms include the freedom to buy and sell what we choose when we choose. Americans also enjoy the freedom to compete, to earn a living, to earn a profit, and to own property.

Americans are free to buy and sell any legal product. Shoppers can search for the best-quality goods and services at the lowest prices. If a price is too high, the buyer is free to look elsewhere for the product.

Producers are generally free to sell goods and services at prices that they think buyers will pay. If people do not buy a product or service, the producer is free to change the price or to sell something else. The term *free market* refers to the exchange between buyers and sellers who are free to choose. The role of the government in the free market is limited.

American businesses compete with one another for customers. That is, each business firm tries to persuade people to buy what it has to offer. In this system of free competition, buyers show which goods and services they favor every time they make a purchase. If consumers do not buy their product, producers will make something else or go out of business. Therefore, producers compete to make what they think the public will buy.

American workers are free to seek the best jobs that their training and education qualifies them to perform. In addition, they may bargain with their employers for higher wages, more benefits, and better working conditions. American workers are free to leave their jobs to find better ones or to start their own businesses.

Profit is the income a business has left after expenses. The profit motive, or desire to make a profit, is essential to a free economic system. It is the reason that people start and operate businesses. It also is the reason that people invest in, or put money into, various businesses and valuable goods.

All Americans are free to do as they like with their own money. They may spend, save, or invest it. They may buy buildings, land, tools, and machines. These forms of property may be used to produce goods and services. That is, Americans may start their own businesses and use them to earn profits.

Under the U.S. economic system, the free market helps determine how Americans use limited resources. People are free to produce, sell, and buy whatever they choose. Of course, businesses would not last long if they produced things that no one wanted. Businesses must supply what buyers in the market demand.

---

1   This selection is mostly about—

   A   the emergence of bartering.

   B   the changing American family.

   C   the American economic system.

   D   shopping in America.

2   Which of the following defines <u>free market</u>?

   F   freedom to buy and sell

   G   freedom to compete

   H   freedom to earn a profit

   J   all of the above

1 Ⓐ Ⓑ Ⓒ Ⓓ
2 Ⓕ Ⓖ Ⓗ Ⓙ

3 What is the role of the government in a free market?

A to control all businesses and consumers

B to regulate where all Americans work

C to protect the freedom of citizens

D to deny businesses the right to sell competitively

4 A producer of a product is generally free to—

F change the price of the product or service.

G pay its workers less than the minimum wage.

H set the price of other businesses' products.

J lie about its product.

5 Because the government does not set a standard price on goods, businesses are free to—

A hurt consumers.

B forget to pay their suppliers.

C take advantage of workers.

D compete with one another on price.

6 According to the passage, why do most people start their own businesses?

F because of the profit motive

G because they think it is exciting

H because they want to be their own boss

J because they like competition

7 What are some of the things Americans do with the money they earn?

A invest it

B spend it

C start their own businesses

D all of the above

8 In your own words, explain some of the economic freedoms Americans possess.

_____

_____

_____

_____

_____

_____

9 Which of the following happens as a result of the profit motive?

A People start and operate businesses.

B People invest in businesses.

C People invest in valuable goods.

D all of the above

10 American workers are free to—

F bargain with their employers on pay.

G seek the best jobs their training and education qualify them for.

H leave their jobs to find better ones.

J all of the above

11 In your own words, write a summary of the benefits of a free-market economy.

_____

_____

_____

_____

_____

_____

3 Ⓐ Ⓑ Ⓒ Ⓓ   5 Ⓐ Ⓑ Ⓒ Ⓓ   7 Ⓐ Ⓑ Ⓒ Ⓓ   9 Ⓐ Ⓑ Ⓒ Ⓓ   11 Open-ended

4 Ⓕ Ⓖ Ⓗ Ⓙ   6 Ⓕ Ⓖ Ⓗ Ⓙ   8 Open-ended   10 Ⓕ Ⓖ Ⓗ Ⓙ

Activity 18 Vocabulary: Goods and Services

Directions: Darken the circle for the correct answer, or write your answer in the space provided.

1 What are <u>machine tools</u>?

  A machinery built to produce parts that are unique

  B machinery built to produce parts that are exactly the same

  C tools made by human hands

  D tools used to make the cotton gin

2 One feature of mass marketing is the one-price system. This means—

  F that the price is determined for the product so that the customer does not have to bargain.

  G everything in the store is one price.

  H customers must bargain for each item they buy.

  J there are many prices for each item.

3 The term <u>division of labor</u> means that—

  A all the labor in the United States is divided equally.

  B in the mass production of products, each worker has a certain part of the job.

  C the United States must share the labor with other countries.

  D none of the above

4 Economists use the gross domestic product (GDP) as one measure of how well the U.S. economy is performing. What is the <u>gross domestic product</u>?

  F the number of all of the goods produced in the United States

  G the number of all of the goods produced in other countries

  H the dollar value of all goods and services produced annually in the United States

  J the cost of all of the goods produced in the United States

5 An <u>installment</u> plan allows a buyer to use a product while paying for it. What does the term <u>installment</u> mean?

  A Consumers have to pay for the item before leaving the place of purchase.

  B The consumer pays more for the product.

  C The price of an item is paid in equal payments over a period of weeks, months, or years.

  D The price of the item is reduced.

6 If a consumer makes incomplete payments on an item, the seller can repossess it. What does <u>repossess</u> mean?

  F The seller destroys the item.

  G The seller takes the item back.

  H The seller resells the item.

  J The seller gives the item to someone else.

1 Ⓐ Ⓑ Ⓒ Ⓓ 3 Ⓐ Ⓑ Ⓒ Ⓓ 5 Ⓐ Ⓑ Ⓒ Ⓓ
2 Ⓕ Ⓖ Ⓗ Ⓙ 4 Ⓕ Ⓖ Ⓗ Ⓙ 6 Ⓕ Ⓖ Ⓗ Ⓙ

7 There are some disadvantages to charge accounts. Because charge accounts are easy to use, some people use them to buy things on impulse that they do not need. What does the word impulse mean?

A acting without thinking

B refusing to worry about bills

C ignoring reality

D acting immaturely

8 A good credit rating is essential when you want to apply for a bank loan or buy a house. What is a credit rating?

F a report that shows how much Americans owe to their creditors

G a report that shows how much a customer has bought on credit

H a report that shows how reliable a customer is in paying bills

J none of the above

9 Banks and credit card companies charge interest on their loans. What is interest?

A money the banks and credit card companies pay the consumer for using their services

B money the banks and credit card companies charge the consumer for the loan

C money the banks collect from manufacturers

D all of the above

10 In your own words, summarize some of the important elements of mass marketing.

_____

_____

_____

_____

11 Florence Kelley helped influence the country by fighting for child labor reform laws and for a minimum wage for all workers. What is a minimum wage?

F the pay an employee receives minus taxes

G the lowest pay the government states an employer must pay his or her employees

H the maximum pay the government states an employer can pay his or her employees

J the pay an employee receives from the government

12 List some reasons that it would be better to pay cash for goods than to charge them.

_____

_____

_____

_____

_____

_____

_____

13 Describe the difference between wholesalers and retailers.

_____

_____

_____

_____

_____

_____

_____

7 Ⓐ Ⓑ Ⓒ Ⓓ   **9** Ⓐ Ⓑ Ⓒ Ⓓ   **11** Ⓕ Ⓖ Ⓗ Ⓙ   **13** Open-ended
8 Ⓕ Ⓖ Ⓗ Ⓙ   **10** Open-ended   **12** Open-ended

Activity 19 Language: Managing Money

Directions: Sean was asked to write a letter explaining currency to a younger student. Please read the rough draft of his essay and answer the following questions.

When you go buy something. You hardly ever think about the currency,
(1)   **(2)**

or money. However, currency, or money, is more complicated than you
(3)

think. A bank considers money to be checks, bank accounts, and other
(4)

forms of paper and electronic wealth. All of the money we use everyday
(5)

is made by the government. Part of the value of the money is based on
(6)

the reserves of wealth controlled by the government. A countrys currency
(7)

has value because it will buy things. Every country in the world has a
(8)

currency. Which is cool if you think about it. All currencies share these
(9)   **(10)**

features; they must be easy to carry, be based on a system of units that

are easy to multiply and divide, be durable, be made in a standard form,

and be guaranteed by the country's government that issues it.

U.S. coins used to have silver and gold in them can you believe that?
(11)

All coins are alloys, or a mixture, of metals now. pennies are copper-
(12)   **(13)**

coated zinc. Nickels dimes quarters, and half-dollars are alloys of copper
(14)

and nickel. The new dollar coins also is a mixture of copper, zinc, and
(15)

other minerals. But most people use checks or their credit cards anyway.
(16)

1 In sentence 10, the semicolon should be a—

A period.

B comma.

C colon.

D question mark.

2 What is sentence 14 missing?

F a capital letter

G a period

H a quotation mark

J commas

3 Which sentence has a subject/verb agreement error?

A 11

B 12

C 14

D 15

4 Where is one of the sentence fragments in the paper?

F 1

G 2

H 3

J 4

5 Which sentence is missing an apostrophe?

A 7

B 8

C 9

D 10

6 Write an appropriate topic sentence for paragraph 2.

_____

_____

_____

_____

7 Describe, in your own words, what currency is.

_____

_____

_____

_____

8 Which sentence does not belong in the second paragraph?

F 13

G 14

H 15

J 16

9 Which is a run-on sentence?

A 11

B 12

C 13

D 14

10 Which sentence is missing a capital letter?

F 11

G 12

H 13

J 14

11 Rewrite the last sentence to be a better closing sentence.

_____

_____

_____

_____

_____

_____

1 Ⓐ Ⓑ Ⓒ Ⓓ   3 Ⓐ Ⓑ Ⓒ Ⓓ   5 Ⓐ Ⓑ Ⓒ Ⓓ   7 Open-ended   9 Ⓐ Ⓑ Ⓒ Ⓓ
2 Ⓕ Ⓖ Ⓗ Ⓙ   4 Ⓕ Ⓖ Ⓗ Ⓙ   6 Open-ended   8 Ⓕ Ⓖ Ⓗ Ⓙ   10 Ⓕ Ⓖ Ⓗ Ⓙ
11 Open-ended

Activity 20 Social Science: Economic Challenges

Directions: Darken the circle for the correct answer, or write your answer in the space provided.

1 When did the Great Depression take place?

   A 1919 through 1929

   B 1929 through the 1930s

   C 1939 through the 1940s

   D 1949 through the 1950s

2 Before the Great Depression, economists believed that—

   F the government should not control inflation, boost production, or end unemployment.

   G the government should control inflation, boost production, and end unemployment.

   H the government should stay out of the affairs of businesses.

   J both F and H

3 What was established as a result of the Great Depression?

   A Social Security

   B the Federal Deposit Insurance Corporation

   C the Securities and Exchange Commission

   D all of the above

4 Inflation occurs when—

   F wages increase faster than prices.

   G prices increase faster than wages.

   H the national debt increases more than revenue.

   J taxes increase, but wages do not.

5 What causes economic problems?

   A unemployment

   B recession

   C inflation

   D all of the above

6 What does the government do to help in an economic recession?

   F increases the money supply by buying back bonds

   G increases the amount of money banks can lend

   H lowers the interest rate that banks must pay the Fed for their loans

   J all of the above

7 What is the purpose of a labor union?

   A to improve working conditions and the wages of workers

   B to improve the profits of the owners of a company

   C to improve the economy

   D to improve education

8 In a closed shop, workers must—

   F not work for unions.

   G work for unions.

   H work for minimum wage.

   J none of the above

1 Ⓐ Ⓑ Ⓒ Ⓓ   3 Ⓐ Ⓑ Ⓒ Ⓓ   5 Ⓐ Ⓑ Ⓒ Ⓓ   7 Ⓐ Ⓑ Ⓒ Ⓓ

2 Ⓕ Ⓖ Ⓗ Ⓙ   4 Ⓕ Ⓖ Ⓗ Ⓙ   6 Ⓕ Ⓖ Ⓗ Ⓙ   8 Ⓕ Ⓖ Ⓗ Ⓙ

9 Featherbedding is a term that describes—

   A union workers striking.

   B labor unions and workers negotiating.

   C a union's forcing employers to hire more workers than are needed.

   D employers hiring more employees than needed and then paying them less.

10 In your own words, describe the function of a labor union.

_____

_____

_____

_____

_____

_____

_____

11 About what percentage of workers in America belong to a union?

   F 20 percent

   G 30 percent

   H 40 percent

   J 50 percent

12 What is mediation?

   A Labor unions suggest solutions.

   B The employer suggests solutions.

   C Neither side will negotiate.

   D During a strike, an expert on relations between labor and management examines the problems and recommends solutions.

13 In President Franklin D. Roosevelt's first inaugural address, he tried to encourage struggling Americans to believe in themselves during the Great Depression. He said, "This great nation will endure as it has endured, will revive and will prosper. So, first of all, let me assert my firm belief that the only thing we have to fear is fear itself." In your own words, write what you think President Roosevelt meant by that statement.

_____

_____

_____

_____

_____

_____

_____

14 In your own words, please write a brief summary of the role of the government in the economy.

_____

_____

_____

_____

_____

_____

_____

_____

   9 Ⓐ Ⓑ Ⓒ Ⓓ   **11** Ⓕ Ⓖ Ⓗ Ⓙ   **13** Open-ended

   10 Open-ended   **12** Ⓐ Ⓑ Ⓒ Ⓓ   **14** Open-ended

NAME _____ CLASS _____ DATE _____

Activity 21 Reading Comprehension: The U.S. Economy and the World

Directions: Darken the circle for the correct answer, or write your answer in the space provided.

International trade allows nations to gain wealth. For many reasons, however, nations often limit the exchange of goods across their borders. A government action that limits the exchange of goods is called a trade barrier. Governments use trade barriers to protect domestic jobs and industries from foreign competition. The major types of trade barriers are tariffs, import quotas, voluntary restrictions, and embargoes.

Goods and services purchased by one nation from another are called imports. A tax on imports is called a tariff. There are two kinds of tariffs. Revenue tariffs are used to raise money for a government. Protective tariffs restrict the number of foreign goods sold in a country. A protective tariff helps domestic industry because it raises the cost of imported goods. Because the foreign goods now cost more, demand will be reduced. Consumers will choose the good that was manufactured domestically instead.

The United States has used protective tariffs for much of its history. Since World War II, the United States has reduced its use of protective tariffs, but it does still place

heavy tariffs on some goods, including Japanese motorcycles and trucks.

Governments also use import quotas and voluntary trade restrictions to limit imports. An import quota is a law that limits the amount or number of a certain import. A voluntary trade restriction is an agreement between two countries, rather than a law. Both of these forms of regulation help domestic businesses. Because the amount of the import is limited, domestic businesses can attract some consumers and their goods.

Import quotas and voluntary trade restrictions are often aimed at specific goods from specific countries. For example, U.S. automobile makers were concerned about the sale of Japanese cars in the United States. As Americans bought Japanese cars, the number of American-made cars dropped. The U.S. government asked the Japanese government to voluntarily limit the number of cars sold in the United States. In 1981 Japan agreed to sell only 1.7 million cars in the United States. Today voluntary trade restrictions no longer exist on Japanese cars.

---

1   This selection is mostly about—

A   automobile makers.

B   how to make money.

C   businesses.

D   international trade.

2   What is a protective tariff?

F   a tax on imported goods

G   a tax on domestic goods

H   a restriction on the number of imported cars

J   a restriction on the number of foreign immigrants

1 Ⓐ Ⓑ Ⓒ Ⓓ
2 Ⓕ Ⓖ Ⓗ Ⓙ

3   According to this passage,
    international trade allows countries
    to—

    A   explore other cultures.
    B   amass wealth.
    C   hurt other countries' economic
        health.
    D   influence the world.

4   What are import quotas?

    F   laws that limit the amount of
        certain imported goods
    G   voluntary trade restrictions
    H   bans on imports
    J   none of the above

5   What is a trade barrier?

    A   a government action that limits the
        exchange of goods with other
        countries
    B   a government action that
        encourages the exchange of goods
        with other countries
    C   a government response to a
        prosperous economy
    D   the response of domestic
        businesses to foreign competitors

6   According to the passage, what is the
    purpose of a revenue tariff?

    F   to encourage trade
    G   to help other countries
    H   to make money
    J   to sell more American products

7   Why do you think that the Japanese
    government would comply with the
    voluntary restriction on Japanese
    cars?

    _____

    _____

    _____

    _____

8   In your own words, explain why
    import quotas are necessary.

    _____

    _____

    _____

    _____

9   Why do some foreign goods cost
    more than the same American goods?

    A   because they are made better
    B   because protective tariffs raise the
        price of the goods
    C   because goods are cheaper in
        America
    D   because American products are
        superior

10 According to the passage, what is
    another reason for trade barriers?

    F   to ensure peace with other
        countries
    G   to ensure the reputation of
        American goods in the world
    H   to ensure Americans' freedom
    J   to ensure domestic jobs

11 Summarize the important points in
    this passage.

    _____

    _____

    _____

    _____

    _____

    _____

    _____

3 Ⓐ Ⓑ Ⓒ Ⓓ   5 Ⓐ Ⓑ Ⓒ Ⓓ   7 Open-ended   9 Ⓐ Ⓑ Ⓒ Ⓓ   11 Open-ended
4 Ⓕ Ⓖ Ⓗ Ⓙ   6 Ⓕ Ⓖ Ⓗ Ⓙ   8 Open-ended   10 Ⓕ Ⓖ Ⓗ Ⓙ

Activity 22 Language: Career Choices

Directions: Samantha was asked to write a report on finding a career. Please read her rough draft and answer the following questions.

Choosing a career can be one of the hardest and most confusing things
(1)

you ever do. Mainly because there are so many to choose from. A good
      (2)   **(3)**

source of information on jobs available in your community is the

classified section of your newspaper, the classified section contains help-

wanted ads listing employment opportunity. Most help wanted ads
                           (4)

follow the same general organization. They are divided into major
                (5)

categories such as accounting/bookkeeping, engineering, medical,

office/clerical, professional, and sales. Note what training or experience
             (6)

is required. Also, note the salary, benefits, or description of professional
     (7)

duties. Note how many jobs are advertised. If a job you are interested in
    (8)   **(9)**

only has one or two ads, think about if it will be likely for you to get a job

in that area. Another way to learn about careers is to read the books, and
     (10)

magazines available on the subject. One of the most helpful sources
      (11)

of information about jobs is the u.s. department of Labor they have

researched many careers to make up the book. Reading about career
     (12)

opportunities to find a career that interests you is like doing detective

work. You can also learn about jobs as they go about your daily affairs.
  (13)

Observe the work of bus drivers, police officers, teachers, office workers,
(14)

and others you meet every day. Be aware of the jobs that you see every-
    (15)

day. There is a job out there that suits you. The hard part is finding it.
  (16)   **(17)**

1 Which sentence is a comma splice?

A 3
B 4
C 6
D 7

2 Which sentence has a term that is missing a hyphen?

F 1
G 2
H 3
J 4

3 Which sentence has a capitalization error?

A 8
B 9
C 10
D 11

4 Where is the sentence fragment in the paper?

F 1
G 2
H 3
J 4

5 In sentence 13, what is incorrect?

A misplaced commas
B punctuation
C spelling
D noun/pronoun agreement

6 Create an appropriate title for Samantha's essay.

_____

_____

_____

_____

7 Combine sentences 15 and 16 into one sentence that is correctly punctuated.

_____

_____

_____

_____

_____

8 Describe, in your own words, how to investigate career options.

_____

_____

_____

_____

_____

9 Which sentence is redundant?

F 14
G 15
H 16
J 17

10 Which sentence is a run-on sentence?

A 11
B 12
C 13
D 14

11 Which sentence would be a good place to begin a new paragraph?

F 8
G 9
H 10
J 11

1 Ⓐ Ⓑ Ⓒ Ⓓ   **3** Ⓐ Ⓑ Ⓒ Ⓓ   **5** Ⓐ Ⓑ Ⓒ Ⓓ   **7** Open-ended   **9** Ⓕ Ⓖ Ⓗ Ⓙ   **11** Ⓕ Ⓖ Ⓗ Ⓙ
2 Ⓕ Ⓖ Ⓗ Ⓙ   **4** Ⓕ Ⓖ Ⓗ Ⓙ   **6** Open-ended   **8** Open-ended   **10** Ⓐ Ⓑ Ⓒ Ⓓ

Activity 23 Vocabulary: Foreign Policy

Directions: Darken the circle for the correct answer, or write your answer in the space provided.

1 What are couriers?

A ambassadors

B politicians

C messengers

D tools

2 Alliances are made up of—

F countries that do not support one another.

G countries that support one another.

H countries that declare war on each other.

J countries that do not have similar economies.

3 Advances in communication and transportation have encouraged the interdependence of the world's countries. The word interdependence means—

A independent

B mutual dependence

C unequal dependence

D none of the above

4 A summit is a—

F meeting of high-level officials.

G meeting of politicians from one country.

H meeting of citizens to promote change.

J meeting of community leaders.

5 The success of the Pacific Rim countries has had a significant effect on the U.S. balance of trade. What is the balance of trade?

A the amount a country exports

B the amount a country imports

C the value of what a country produces

D the difference in the value of a country's exports and imports over a period of time

6 NAFTA allows free trade between the United States, Canada, and Mexico. The term free trade means—

F trade that is restricted by tariffs and other barriers.

G trade that is not restricted by tariffs and other barriers.

H trade that is illegal.

J goods that are exchanged for free between countries.

7 The United States has helped countries in Africa, Asia, and Latin America become self-sufficient. What does the term self-sufficient mean?

A having to rely on others

B being able to take care of oneself

C being able to take care of others

D not caring about others

1 Ⓐ Ⓑ Ⓒ Ⓓ   3 Ⓐ Ⓑ Ⓒ Ⓓ   5 Ⓐ Ⓑ Ⓒ Ⓓ   7 Ⓐ Ⓑ Ⓒ Ⓓ

2 Ⓕ Ⓖ Ⓗ Ⓙ   4 Ⓕ Ⓖ Ⓗ Ⓙ   6 Ⓕ Ⓖ Ⓗ Ⓙ

8 The breakup of the Soviet Union and the move toward democracy in Eastern Europe has <u>renewed</u> interest in NATO. What does word <u>renewed</u> mean?

F   to refuse

G   to end

H   to begin again

J   none of the above

9 An important part of U.S. foreign policy is <u>foreign aid</u>. What is <u>foreign aid</u>?

A   a government program that provides economic or military assistance to another country

B   help provided by Americans living in foreign countries

C   money that the banks lend to other countries

D   all of the above

10 What are some of the Department of State's duties?

_____

_____

_____

_____

_____

_____

_____

_____

_____

11 The United States participates in <u>humanitarian</u> efforts. What does the word <u>humanitarian</u> mean?

F   helping foreign countries in war

G   helping businesses succeed

H   helping governments rule effectively

J   helping human beings in their daily lives

12 Describe the <u>United Nations</u> in your own words.

_____

_____

_____

_____

_____

_____

_____

13 What is an <u>executive agreement</u> between countries?

_____

_____

_____

_____

_____

_____

_____

8 Ⓕ Ⓖ Ⓗ Ⓙ   **10** Open-ended   **12** Open-ended

9 Ⓐ Ⓑ Ⓒ Ⓓ   **11** Ⓕ Ⓖ Ⓗ Ⓙ   **13** Open-ended

Activity 24 Language: Charting a Course

Directions: Mike was asked to write a paper explaining the end of the Cold War. Please read his rough draft and answer the questions below.

The Cold War refers to the tensions between the United States and the
(1)

Soviet Union. Nearly every country in the world was affected by both
                    (2)

countries race to secure alliances and to build their weapons capabilities.

In 1985, after years of distrust and hostility. Mikhail Gorbachev
(3)   **(4)**

became the leader of the Soviet Union. He was faced with a failing
                                        (5)

economy and unhappy citizens. Two years after Gorbachev was in office,
                        (6)

he introduced a policy called glasnonst, or openness. Gorbachevs other
                                                        (7)

program perestroika was aimed at improving the Soviet economy. In
                                                                (8)

1987 the two countries signed a treaty agreeing to remove their medium-

range nuclear weapons from Europe. Encouraged by Soviet reforms,
                                        (9)

citizens in a number of Eastern European countries demanded

democracy and free elections. These citizens demanded democracy and
                                        (10)

free elections, this act changed the world. Six Eastern European countries
                            (11)

fell the world was astonished. The Berlin Wall, built in 1961, to separate
                    (12)

communist East Berlin from democratic West Berlin, was taken down.

The soviets opened local elections to parties other than the Communist
(13)

party for the first time. In 1990 pro-democracy candidates won many of
                            (14)

these elections. The Commonwealth of Independent States replaced the
                    (15)

Soviet Union.

1 In sentence 10, the comma should be replaced by—

  A quotation marks.

  B a hyphen.

  C a colon.

  D a period or semicolon.

2 Which sentence has a misspelled foreign term?

  F 6

  G 7

  H 13

  J 15

3 Which sentence would be a good place to begin a new paragraph?

  A 10

  B 11

  C 13

  D 14

4 Where is one of the sentence fragments in the paper?

  F 1

  G 2

  H 3

  J 4

5 Which sentence is missing an apostrophe?

  A 7

  B 8

  C 9

  D 10

6 Create an appropriate title for Mike's essay.

_____

_____

_____

7 Combine sentences 3 and 4 into one sentence that is correctly punctuated.

_____

_____

_____

_____

8 Describe the Cold War in your own words.

_____

_____

_____

_____

_____

9 Which is a run-on sentence?

  F 11

  G 12

  H 13

  J 14

10 Which sentence is missing a capital letter?

  A 11

  B 12

  C 13

  D 14

11 Write an appropriate closing sentence for this paper.

_____

_____

_____

_____

1 Ⓐ Ⓑ Ⓒ Ⓓ   **3** Ⓐ Ⓑ Ⓒ Ⓓ   **5** Ⓐ Ⓑ Ⓒ Ⓓ   **7** Open-ended   **9** Ⓕ Ⓖ Ⓗ Ⓙ   **11** Open-ended

2 Ⓕ Ⓖ Ⓗ Ⓙ   **4** Ⓕ Ⓖ Ⓗ Ⓙ   **6** Open-ended   **8** Open-ended   **10** Ⓐ Ⓑ Ⓒ Ⓓ

Activity 25 Social Science: Improving Life for All Americans

Directions: Darken the circle for the correct answer, or write your answer in the space provided.

1 **Why did the population move from cities to the suburbs?**

    A crime rates

    B air quality

    C jobs

    D all of the above

2 **What happens to urban areas when the population moves to the suburbs?**

    F Businesses leave the area.

    G Unemployment in urban areas rises.

    H The cities become more run-down.

    J all of the above

3 **Approximately how many Americans have been homeless at some time in their lives?**

    A 1 million

    B 5 million

    C 7 million

    D 13 million

4 **Mass transit is—**

    F walking to work.

    G car pooling.

    H transportation that serves many passengers at once.

    J commuters driving their cars.

5 **What is a minority group?**

    A a group of people who work together

    B a group that does not have as much political or economic power as other groups

    C a group that has the most political and economic power in society

    D none of the above

6 **Throughout America's history, some people have been discriminated against because they belong to a particular cultural, ethnic, or religious group. What does discriminated against mean?**

    F fairly treated by others

    G unfairly treated by others

    H treated kindly

    J treated with favoritism

7 **What is a boycott?**

    A buying or using a business's goods or services because of its fair treatment of people

    B refusing to buy or use a business's goods or services because of its business practices

    C disobeying laws that you believe to be wrong

    D taking unfair actions against a minority group

1 Ⓐ Ⓑ Ⓒ Ⓓ   **3** Ⓐ Ⓑ Ⓒ Ⓓ   **5** Ⓐ Ⓑ Ⓒ Ⓓ   **7** Ⓐ Ⓑ Ⓒ Ⓓ

2 Ⓕ Ⓖ Ⓗ Ⓙ   **4** Ⓕ Ⓖ Ⓗ Ⓙ   **6** Ⓕ Ⓖ Ⓗ Ⓙ

8 What is <u>segregation</u>?

    F uniting the races

    G separating the races

    H including all races

    J denying one race the right to vote

9 Civil rights refer to—

    A the right to equal treatment under the law.

    B the right to use public places and facilities.

    C the right to vote and to an equal education.

    D all of the above

10 In your own words, describe the prejudice that some groups of Americans—such as Catholics, American Indians, and African Americans—have experienced in our country's history.

_____

_____

_____

_____

_____

_____

_____

_____

_____

11 What did the court case *Brown* v. *Board of Education of Topeka* concern?

    F voting rights of African Americans

    G fair treatment of African American teachers

    H segregation in schools

    J unfair treatment of African American workers

12 What is <u>civil disobedience</u>?

    A showing dissent by intentionally disobeying laws

    B rioting in the streets

    C boycotting businesses

    D picketing an organization

13 In your own words, describe what Rosa Parks did for the civil rights movement.

_____

_____

_____

_____

_____

14 In your own words, describe some of the protest methods that have been used effectively to bring about change and to help end discrimination.

_____

_____

_____

_____

_____

8 Ⓕ Ⓖ Ⓗ Ⓙ **10** Open-ended **12** Ⓐ Ⓑ Ⓒ Ⓓ **14** Open-ended
9 Ⓐ Ⓑ Ⓒ Ⓓ **11** Ⓕ Ⓖ Ⓗ Ⓙ **13** Open-ended

Activity 26 Reading Comprehension: The Global Environment

Directions: Darken the circle for the correct answer, or write your answer in the space provided.

The air we breathe is a mixture of nitrogen, oxygen, carbon dioxide, and small amounts of other gases. It is a renewable resource and can therefore be replaced. Dirt and harmful gases released by furnaces, factories, and automobiles cause air pollution. Under normal conditions, natural processes clean pollution from the air. However, in recent years this air pollution has become so great that nature cannot easily get rid of it.

The air over many of the world's cities is filled with smog—a combination of smoke, gases, and fog. Smog burns the eyes and lungs. High levels of smog can be harmful to human health. A 1995 study found that people living in U.S. cities with high levels of air pollution are more likely to die at younger ages than people living in the country's cleanest cities.

Air pollution has caused other problems as well. Over the last hundred years, the levels of carbon dioxide and other gases released into the atmosphere has risen dramatically. At the same time, millions of acres of forests, whose trees absorb carbon dioxide, have been destroyed. Some scientists believe that the resulting high level of carbon dioxide causes Earth's atmosphere to absorb more of the Sun's heat. For million of years, Earth's atmosphere has naturally absorbed the Sun's rays and maintained a temperature that made the planet habitable for life. However, some scientists believe that increased carbon dioxide in Earth's atmosphere raises the temperature. This process creates a greenhouse effect.

The greenhouse effect is of concern because it may lead to global warming, a general increase in Earth's temperature. This warming could have devastating effects on the environment. It could change global climates and weather patterns and possibly destroy ecosystems. The issue of global warming is still controversial. Much of the research on global warming is based on computer models that simulate Earth's environment. Some scientists have argued that Earth's atmosphere is too complicated to accurately model in a computer simulation.

Another problem posed by air pollution is that it thins Earth's ozone layer. The ozone layer is a thin layer in Earth's upper atmosphere that shields the planet from the Sun's ultraviolet rays. These rays can be dangerous to living things.

1 **This selection is mostly about—**

   A the galaxy.

   B the atmosphere.

   C air pollution.

   D the debates among scientists.

2 **What is smog?**

   F the ozone layer

   G harmful rays from the Sun

   H a combination of smoke, gases, and fog

   J a form of acid rain

1 Ⓐ Ⓑ Ⓒ Ⓓ
2 Ⓕ Ⓖ Ⓗ Ⓙ

3 What do some scientists believe causes global warming?

A destruction of forests

B pollution

C both A and B

D none of the above

4 What does the atmosphere do for Earth?

F absorbs the Sun's heat and makes the planet habitable

G absorbs pollution

H absorbs volcanic ash

J absorbs water

5 What is the ozone layer?

A the entire atmosphere

B a layer of earth that absorbs water

C a thin layer in Earth's upper atmosphere that shields the planet from the Sun's ultraviolet rays

D a body of water that absorbs the Sun's rays

6 Why are trees important to the environment?

F They absorb carbon dioxide.

G They absorb oxygen.

H They absorb nitrogen.

J They absorb ultraviolet rays.

7 Why is global warming controversial?

A Businesses do not want to make their factories pollution-free.

B Some scientists do not accept the research because most of it is based on computer models of Earth's environment.

C Scientists never agree on anything.

D People do not want to believe that anything bad can happen to the environment.

8 In your own words, describe why human beings should care about the environment.

_____

_____

_____

_____

_____

_____

9 What are the negative effects of pollution on humans and the environment?

_____

_____

_____

_____

_____

_____

10 What are the gases in the air that we breathe?

F oxygen

G nitrogen

H carbon dioxide

J all of the above

11 What do some scientists believe will result from global warming?

A Plants and animals could die.

B Ecosystems could be destroyed.

C Humans could suffer.

D all of the above

3 Ⓐ Ⓑ Ⓒ Ⓓ   5 Ⓐ Ⓑ Ⓒ Ⓓ   7 Ⓐ Ⓑ Ⓒ Ⓓ   9 Open-ended   11 Ⓐ Ⓑ Ⓒ Ⓓ
4 Ⓕ Ⓖ Ⓗ Ⓙ   6 Ⓕ Ⓖ Ⓗ Ⓙ   8 Open-ended   10 Ⓕ Ⓖ Ⓗ Ⓙ

Part 2: Practice Tests

Practice Test 1: Reading Comprehension

Sample A

State legislators sometimes draw district lines that favor a particular political party, politician, or group of people. This practice is called gerrymandering. For example, a state legislature made up mostly of Democrats might draw district lines that place Democratic voters in a majority in as many districts as possible.

When a political party is accused of gerrymandering, it has—

A   voted against its constituents.

B   drawn district lines that favor its party.

C   accepted bribes.

D   rigged the election.

The answer is <u>B</u>.

For questions 1–38, read each selection carefully. Darken the circle for the correct answer, or write your answer in the space provided.

Committees in Congress

Every year Congress has to consider thousands of bills, or proposed laws. Members of the first Congress might have read each of the 268 bills they considered. Today Congress handles about 8,000 bills in a two-year term. It would be impossible for all members of each house to consider every bill that is proposed. Therefore, the members divide their work among many smaller groups, or committees.

Most of the work of Congress is done in committees. The congressional committees study all bills before they are considered by Congress. To obtain information needed to do their work, committees hold hearings and special meetings and conduct investigations.

Each house of Congress has a number of permanent committees, or standing committees. The Senate has 16 standing committees and the House has 19. Each committee is responsible for a special area of congressional business. In the House, for example, the Ways and Means Committee handles all matters concerning taxes. In the Senate, bills related to taxes go to the Finance Committee.

Before Congress considers a bill, it is studied carefully by a standing committee. The committee holds hearings to gain information on the positive and negative aspects of a bill. Committee members may also revise a bill. It is then sent to the entire membership for consideration, along with the committee's recommendation for or against it. The recommendation usually determines whether the members will or will not approve the bill.

1 This selection is mostly about—

A the executive branch of government.

B the committees of Congress.

C the legislative branch of government.

D the president.

2 What is the main function of committees?

F to balance the presidential power

G to make laws for the country

H to study all bills before they are considered by Congress.

J to help people

3 Approximately how many bills does Congress review in a two-year term?

A 2,000

B 4,000

C 6,000

D 8,000

4 What is a standing committee?

F representatives from a particular state

G a group of lawyers

H a permanent committee

J a law

5 How many standing committees are there in the Senate?

A 19

B 10

C 16

D 20

6 The committee holds hearings to—

F serve the Supreme Court.

G keep the legislative branch in check.

H decide court cases.

J gain information about the bill.

7 What does the Ways and Means Committee handle?

A all matters concerning taxes

B all matters concerning laws

C all matters concerning public health

D all matters concerning education

8 Why are committees necessary to Congress?

_____

_____

_____

_____

9 How do the recommendations of a committee influence members of Congress?

F The recommendation usually determines whether the members will or will not approve the bill.

G The recommendation carries little weight on whether or not the members will or will not approve the bill.

H The recommendation influences how voters see the issue.

J none of the above

1 Ⓐ Ⓑ Ⓒ Ⓓ   3 Ⓐ Ⓑ Ⓒ Ⓓ   5 Ⓐ Ⓑ Ⓒ Ⓓ   7 Ⓐ Ⓑ Ⓒ Ⓓ   9 Ⓕ Ⓖ Ⓗ Ⓙ
2 Ⓕ Ⓖ Ⓗ Ⓙ   4 Ⓕ Ⓖ Ⓗ Ⓙ   6 Ⓕ Ⓖ Ⓗ Ⓙ   8 Open-ended

A Diverse Population

People from all over the world have influenced the development of the United States population. Today's Americans come from many different cultural backgrounds and represent a wide variety of ethnic groups. However, they are united by a common bond—they are all Americans.

Hispanics are the country's largest minority group. This group has seen tremendous growth since 1980. Hispanics number more than 35 million and make up 12.5 percent of the population. African Americans are the second-largest minority group. The 34.7 million African Americans living in the United States today make up 12.3 percent of the population. The fastest-growing minority group is the third-largest group—Asian Americans. This group makes up 3.6 percent of the population. From 1990 to 2000, the Asian American population has increased almost 48.3 percent—to more than 10.2 million. Much of this growth took place as a result of immigration.

Recent statistics also show that other changes are taking place in the U.S. population. The size of U.S. households has decreased since 1970. Many couples are having fewer children. Many people, too, now live alone. As a result, today there are more households with fewer people living in them. From 1970 to 2000 the total number of households increased from about 63 million to more than 105 million. The average number of people living in a household declined from more than three people to fewer than three people.

Another change taking place is the increase in the number of single-parent households. From 1970 to 2000, the number of single-parent families in the United States increased from 7 million to 16.5 million. Divorces often lead to women becoming the primary income earner. In general, women remain responsible for child care. Today fewer than 25 percent of the country's households include the traditional family of mother, father, and one or more children.

Changes also have taken place in the roles of men and women. Perhaps one of the most significant changes is that more families have both parents working outside the home. In recent years in the United States, more women than men have been entering and graduating from college. After receiving their education, a greater percentage of women have been entering the American workforce.

In 1970 about 31 million women worked outside the home. Today that number has risen to 65 million. Estimates show that this number will be nearly 75.5 million by the year 2008. Most women work for the same reason that men do—economic necessity.

---

10 This selection is mostly about—

    A divorce.

    B immigrants.

    C single-parent families.

    D the changing American population.

11 What percentage of the population is Hispanic?

    F 10 percent

    G 12.3 percent

    H 12.5 percent

    J 13 percent

---

10 (A) (B) (C) (D)
11 (F) (G) (H) (J)

NAME _____ CLASS _____ DATE _____

12 **What is the fastest-growing minority group in the United States?**

A   African Americans

B   Hispanics

C   Asian Americans

D   none of the above

13 **What was the rate of increase in this group's population from 1990 to 2000?**

F   38 percent

G   48.3 percent

H   50.1 percent

J   60.5 percent

14 **Since 1970, the size of the U.S. household has—**

A   increased.

B   decreased.

C   stayed the same.

D   doubled.

15 **Generally, who remains responsible for child care in this country?**

F   the public schools

G   men

H   women

J   grandparents

16 **In 1970 to 2000, the number of single-parent households increased from seven million to—**

A   10.2 million

B   15.3 million

C   16.5 million

D   20.1 million

17 **In your own words, describe several ways the American family has changed in the last 30 years.**

_____

_____

_____

_____

_____

_____

18 **How has the American workforce changed?**

F   More men are working than women.

G   More women have been graduating from college and entering the workforce.

H   More people are working with college degrees.

J   none of the above

19 **Why are more women working?**

A   because they can

B   because the workforce needs them

C   out of economic necessity

D   because they are bored at home

20 **In 1970 about 31 million women worked; however, today nearly—**

F   40 million women work.

G   55 million women work.

H   60 million women work.

J   65 million women work.

12 Ⓐ Ⓑ Ⓒ Ⓓ   14 Ⓐ Ⓑ Ⓒ Ⓓ   16 Ⓐ Ⓑ Ⓒ Ⓓ   18 Ⓕ Ⓖ Ⓗ Ⓙ   20 Ⓕ Ⓖ Ⓗ Ⓙ
13 Ⓕ Ⓖ Ⓗ Ⓙ   15 Ⓕ Ⓖ Ⓗ Ⓙ   17 Open-ended   19 Ⓐ Ⓑ Ⓒ Ⓓ

Providing for Change

One of the most important features of the U.S. Constitution is its flexibility. The framers of the Constitution knew that the plan of government they were creating would have to meet the needs of a growing nation.

They could not possibly foresee all the changes the United States would undergo. Yet the government established by the Constitution has been able to adapt to new circumstances and challenges. There are three ways in which the Constitution and the government can be adapted to the changing needs and conditions of the country—through amendment, interpretation, and custom.

An amendment is a written change made to the Constitution. The process for amending, or changing, the Constitution is set forth in Article V of the Constitution.

It is not easy to amend the Constitution. All proposed amendments require the approval of three fourths of the states. Securing this approval for an amendment may take a long time. As a result, it is likely that careful consideration will be given to a proposed amendment before it is passed. Since the Constitution went into effect in 1789, only 27 amendments have been added to it.

An amendment may be proposed in two ways. Both the U.S. Congress and the states must be involved in either process. The first way allows Congress to propose an amendment by a two-thirds vote in both houses. Because a two-thirds vote in Congress is difficult to obtain, members should be certain that the amendment is needed.

The second way of proposing an amendment to the Constitution begins with the states. Using this method, the legislatures of two thirds of the states—34 out of 50—can ask Congress to call a national convention to propose an amendment. This method has never been used successfully. However, it could be used if Congress should refuse to propose an amendment that a large number of Americans believe is necessary.

After an amendment has been proposed, it must then be ratified, or approved, by three fourths, or 38, of the states. There are two ways an amendment may be ratified. The method of ratification used must be described in each proposed amendment.

One method involves sending the proposed amendment to the state legislatures for approval. All but one of the amendments to the Constitution were approved this way. The second method involves sending the proposed amendment to the state conventions for consideration. The people of each state elect their state's members.

After an amendment has been ratified by the required number of states, it becomes part of the written Constitution. What happens if the people decide they do not like the effects of an amendment? In that case, the amendment in question can be repealed, or canceled, by another amendment.

21 This selection is mostly about—

A the changing American society.

B the U.S. Constitution's flexibility.

C the way to amend a law.

D the need for change.

22 An amendment is—

A a new idea.

B a court case.

C a committee in Congress.

D a written change made to the Constitution.

23 Why is it necessary for the United States to have a Constitution that is flexible?

A because Americans like change

B because people get tired of the way things were in the past

C so that it can adapt to new circumstances and challenges

D because politicians like to improve things

24 After an amendment has been proposed, it must then be—

F ratified.

G reviewed by the Supreme Court.

H voted on by the general public.

J read by the president.

25 How is an amendment to the Constitution proposed in Congress?

F by a one-third vote

G by a two-thirds vote

H by a unanimous vote

J none of the above

26 What must be described in each proposed amendment?

F the method of informing citizens of the new law

G the method of repeal

H the method of ratification

J the method of informing the Supreme Court justices

27 What year did the U.S. Constitution go into effect?

A 1680

B 1789

C 1800

D 1889

28 In your own words, describe the two ways an amendment may be proposed in Congress.

_____

_____

_____

_____

_____

_____

_____

21 Ⓐ Ⓑ Ⓒ Ⓓ   23 Ⓐ Ⓑ Ⓒ Ⓓ   25 Ⓐ Ⓑ Ⓒ Ⓓ   27 Ⓐ Ⓑ Ⓒ Ⓓ
22 Ⓕ Ⓖ Ⓗ Ⓙ   24 Ⓕ Ⓖ Ⓗ Ⓙ   26 Ⓕ Ⓖ Ⓗ Ⓙ   28 Open-ended

29 How many states must ratify an amendment to make it a law?

F 28

G 38

H 48

J 50

30 How many amendments have been added to the Constitution?

A 17

B 21

C 27

D 37

31 The U.S. Constitution has been described as a "living document." In your own words, describe what this means.

_____

_____

_____

_____

_____

_____

32 What article of the Constitution sets forth the amending process?

F Article I

G Article III

H Article IV

J Article V

33 In your own words, explain why it is difficult to amend the Constitution.

_____

_____

_____

_____

_____

_____

34 What does the term repealed mean in this passage?

A thrown out

B canceled

C erased

D none of the above

35 How were most of the proposed amendments approved?

F by a two-thirds vote of Congress

G by a two-thirds vote of state legislatures

H by the Supreme Court

J by the president

36 Who elects the members of the state legislature?

A the governors of the state

B the senators of the state

C the people of each state

D the vice president of the United States

37 In your own words, summarize the important points of this passage.

_____

_____

_____

_____

_____

38 Why would citizens of the United States want to repeal an amendment?

F because they do not like or approve of the effects of the amendment

G because they have no regard for the situation

H because their senator thinks the repeal should be made

J because the president thinks the repeal should be made

37 Open-ended
38 Ⓕ Ⓖ Ⓗ Ⓙ

Practice Test 2: Reading Vocabulary

Directions: Darken the circle for the correct answer, or write your answer in the space provided.

Sample A

The president <u>promoted</u> his plan for reforming campaign funding. The word <u>promoted</u> in this passage means—

A publicized.

B denied.

C refuted.

D criticized.

The correct answer is <u>A</u>.

---

1 The foreign ambassador <u>insinuated</u> that there was tension between the countries. What does the word <u>insinuated</u> mean?

A stated

B hinted

C made reference to

D all the above

2 When a politician has <u>foresight</u>, he or she has—

F a kind disposition.

G a clear understanding of the future.

H an arrogant attitude.

J bad vision.

3 The House of Commons accepted a strongly worded motion against the <u>continuance</u> of the war with America. The word <u>continuance</u> means—

A beginning.

B ending.

C prolongation.

D none of the above.

4 In an economic <u>depression</u> jobs are hard to find. In which sentence does <u>depression</u> have the same meaning?

F When there was no snow day, the students and teachers fell into a depression.

G A period of depression in the United States has an effect on economies worldwide.

H Sue was relieved to talk about her depression to her mother.

J both F and H

5 Thomas Jefferson thought that in order for a democracy to operate <u>effectively</u>, its citizens had to be educated. What does the word <u>effectively</u> mean?

A producing a positive result

B producing a negative result

C producing a sad result

D producing an interesting result

1 Ⓐ Ⓑ Ⓒ Ⓓ   3 Ⓐ Ⓑ Ⓒ Ⓓ   5 Ⓐ Ⓑ Ⓒ Ⓓ

2 Ⓕ Ⓖ Ⓗ Ⓙ   4 Ⓕ Ⓖ Ⓗ Ⓙ

6 Thomas Jefferson defended the right of the people to rule the country when he said, "It is my opinion that the will of the Majority should always prevail." What does the word prevail mean?

F triumph

G lose

H fail

J defeat

7 Martin Luther King Jr. was influential in abolishing segregation in this country. What does the word influential mean?

A ineffective

B powerful

C powerless

D immobilized

8 A free-enterprise system helps ensure that efficient businesses continue operating and inefficient business do not. The term efficient means—

F competent.

G well organized.

H capable.

J all of the above.

9 American businesspeople are generally free to run their own businesses in the way they think best. They depend on their own enterprise, not the government, to tell them how to operate. Enterprise means—

A initiative.

B rules.

C laws.

D none of the above.

10 In your own words, describe what supply and demand mean in a free-market economy.

_____

_____

_____

_____

_____

_____

11 Federal court judges can be removed from office only by impeachment by Congress. What does impeachment mean?

F to fire

G to challenge or discredit someone in a court of law

H to make retire

J to promote

12 One reason that judges are appointed for life at a fixed salary is to avoid potential obligation to a particular individual or group's point of view. This helps them maintain impartiality. What does impartiality mean?

A neutrality

B bias

C prejudice

D none of the above

6 Ⓕ Ⓖ Ⓗ Ⓙ   8 Ⓕ Ⓖ Ⓗ Ⓙ   10 Open-ended   12 Ⓐ Ⓑ Ⓒ Ⓓ

7 Ⓐ Ⓑ Ⓒ Ⓓ   9 Ⓐ Ⓑ Ⓒ Ⓓ   11 Ⓕ Ⓖ Ⓗ Ⓙ

13 Public education costs American taxpayers around $326 billion a year, including <u>expenditures</u> by the federal government of about $22 billion. What does the word <u>expenditures</u> mean in this sentence?

F taxes

G investments

H profits

J spending

14 There are 12 U.S. courts of appeals. Each court of appeals covers its own <u>circuit</u>. In your own words, describe what a <u>circuit</u> is.

_____

_____

_____

_____

_____

15 Describe what an <u>appeal</u> is in a court of law.

_____

_____

_____

_____

_____

_____

_____

16 Comprehensive high schools offer college preparatory work as well as technical or <u>vocational</u> courses. In this passage, <u>vocational</u> means—

A career training.

B basic skills.

C mathematics.

D none of the above

17 Ruth Ann Minner became Delaware's first female governor in 2000. Her commitment to adult education and child welfare is <u>venerable</u>. What does the word <u>venerable</u> mean?

F scorned

G admired

H celebrated

J refuted

18 Alan Greenspan, chairman of the Federal Reserve, wrote, "Education is a <u>critical</u> issue for our country, and economic education is of particular concern to those of us at the Federal Reserve." What does the word <u>critical</u> mean in this passage?

A very important

B unimportant

C unnecessary

D nonessential

19 Longer life expectancies and lower birthrates mean that an ever-increasing <u>segment</u> of the population will be made up of people of retirement age. What does the word <u>segment</u> mean?

F sector

G piece

H part of

J all of the above

20 When the Social Security Act was passed in 1935, unemployment was a serious problem. The Social Security Act contained a plan to help workers who lost their jobs due to circumstances beyond their control and allowed for unemployment <u>compensation</u>. What does <u>compensation</u> mean?

_____

_____

_____

_____

21 Michael F. Easley of North Carolina stated in his inaugural address, "Good government is not about Democrats and Republicans. It is about children, seniors and working families. You put them first. You are the first Legislature of the new century." Write in your own words what Easley meant.

_____

_____

_____

_____

22 Comprehensive health insurance is not available to most Americans. The word <u>comprehensive</u> means—

A incomplete

B complete

C partial

D nonessential

23 The Bill of Rights calls for <u>separation</u> of church and state. What does the word <u>separation</u> mean in this sense?

F union

G combination

H division

J unification

24 In the United States, political parties are voluntary. What does this statement mean?

_____

_____

_____

_____

25 The protection from <u>unreasonable</u> search and seizure is a right of every American. What does <u>unreasonable</u> mean?

A deserved

B unwarranted

C provoked

D none of the above

19 Ⓕ Ⓖ Ⓗ Ⓙ   **21** Open-ended   **23** Ⓕ Ⓖ Ⓗ Ⓙ   **25** Ⓐ Ⓑ Ⓒ Ⓓ
20 Open-ended   **22** Ⓐ Ⓑ Ⓒ Ⓓ   **24** Open-ended

Practice Test 3: Language

Directions: Connie was asked to write an opinion paper supporting the concept that all citizens of the United States should be taxed according to their income. Read Connie's essay and darken the circle for the correct answer, or write your answer in the space provided.

No country run without money. The united states system of paying taxes
(1)   **(2)**

is based on individual income. Some people think that everyone should
(3)

pay the exact amount of money for taxes. I don't. I think that people
(4)   **(5)**

should be taxed according to how much income they make every year,

that is only fair. Think about it if someone makes $20,000 a year, they
(6)

should not be expected to pay as much as a person who makes $300,000 a

year. Some people say that it should be equal, but it is equal if we each
(7)

pay a certain percentage. Paying taxes is essential to our government.
(8)

taxes pay for our military, roads, schools, the salaries of the politicians.
(9)

Their are several types of taxes. City, state, and federal. There is
(10)   **(11)**   **(12)**

something called sales tax too. My mom said that no one likes to pay
(13)

taxes, but that we all appreciate having good schools, and roads, and a

military when we need it. I guess she is right. Although I won't tell her
(14)   **(15)**

she is.

Sample

What is a major problem with Connie's essay?

  A Connie changes her topic several times.

  B The paper is not about taxes at all.

  C The paper contends we should not pay taxes.

  D none of the above
The correct answer is <u>A</u>.

1   **What sentence is Connie's thesis statement?**

  A 2   **C** 4

  B 3   **D** 5

2   **Which sentence has a subject/verb agreement error?**

  F 1   **H** 3

  G 2   **J** 4

SA Ⓐ Ⓑ Ⓒ Ⓓ   **2** Ⓕ Ⓖ Ⓗ Ⓙ
1 Ⓐ Ⓑ Ⓒ Ⓓ

3 Where is a sentence fragment in the paper?

    A 11

    B 12

    C 13

    D 14

4 Where should there be a paragraph break in the first paragraph?

    F sentence 7

    G sentence 8

    H sentence 9

    J sentence 10

5 Create an appropriate title for Connie's essay in the space provided.

_____

6 Combine sentences 10 and 11 into one sentence that is correctly punctuated.

_____

_____

_____

7 Write in your own words how the federal government of the United States taxes citizens.

_____

_____

_____

8 In Sentence 10, "Their," should be written as—

    A There.

    B They are.

    C The.

    D They're.

9 What sentence is not necessary?

    F 11

    G 12

    H 13

    J 14

10 What is wrong in sentence 2?

    A capitalization error

    B subject/verb agreement

    C misspelling

    D missing period

11 Replace Connie's three concluding sentences with one or two sentences that better sum up this report.

_____

_____

_____

_____

_____

3 Ⓐ Ⓑ Ⓒ Ⓓ   **5** Open-ended   **7** Open-ended   **9** Ⓕ Ⓖ Ⓗ Ⓙ   **11** Open-ended

4 Ⓕ Ⓖ Ⓗ Ⓙ   **6** Open-ended   **8** Ⓐ Ⓑ Ⓒ Ⓓ   **10** Ⓐ Ⓑ Ⓒ Ⓓ

Directions: Tom was asked to write a report on the dangers of monopolies to a free-market economy. Read Tom's essay and darken the circle for the correct answer, or write your answer in the space provided.

One unfair practice used by big business owners is the forming of monopolies.
(1)

A company has a monopoly if it is the only firm selling a product or providing
(2)

a service. If there is no competition for the product or service, the monopolist
(3)

controls the price of the goods. This is particularly dangerous when the product
(4)

is a necessity, such as food. People are then forced to pay the asking price in
(5)

order to acquire the product or service, this is unfair. A merger occurs when
(6)

two or more companies combine to form one company. Which may lead to the
(7)

forming of a monopoly. If all the companies in an industry merge, a monopoly
(8)

forms. One way to cease a monopoly is to form a trust. A trust is several
(9)   **(10)**

companies combining, there is a board of trustees. Each company remains a
(11)

separate business, but the board of trustees makes sure the companies no

longer compete with one another If all the companies in an industry became
(12)

part of the trust a monopoly is created. Once a monopoly is created, the large
(13)

company forces the small companies out of businez by lowering their prices.

Once the little business is bankrupt, the big company can then charge
(14)

whatever they like for their product. This is no way for our countrys businesses
(15)

to run. I think people who create a monopoly should be sent to prison.
(16)

12 What sentence contains a comma splice?

    F 6

    G 7

    H 8

    J 10

13 What sentence is a fragment?

    A 2

    B 3

    C 4

    D 7

14 What would be a good title for Tom's essay?

    F The Unfair Monopolies in a Free Market

    G Big Problems in Big Business

    H Trustees Cannot be Trusted

    J none of the above

15 What is sentence 11 missing?

    A a subject and a verb

    B a period

    C a capital letter

    D a comma

16 Where could Tom begin a new paragraph?

    F sentence 7

    G sentence 8

    H sentence 9

    J sentence 10

17 What is wrong with sentence 16?

    A Tom begins a new topic.

    B Tom is too harsh with people who start monopolies.

    C The sentence is a comma splice.

    D The sentence is punctuated incorrectly.

18 What sentence is missing an apostrophe?

    F 13

    G 14

    H 15

    J 16

19 What is wrong with sentence 13?

    A misuse of pronoun

    B incorrect use of capitalization

    C misspelled word

    D incorrect use of comma

20 In your own words, describe what a monopoly is.

    _____

    _____

    _____

    _____

    _____

21 What is Tom's thesis?

    F Monopolies are an important part of big business.

    G Monopolies are good for a free-market economy.

    H Monopolies are an unfair business practice that goes against the principles of a free-market economy.

    J Monopolies create competition.

22 Which sentence is missing a comma?

    A 11

    B 12

    C 13

    D 14

Practice Test 4: Social Science

Directions: Darken the circle for the correct answer, or write your answer in the space provided.

Sample A

One of the most important features of the U.S. Constitution is its flexibility. The framers of the Constitution knew that the plan of government they were creating would have to meet the needs of a growing nation. They could not possibly foresee all of the changes the United States would undergo. Yet the government established by the Constitution has been able to adapt to new circumstances and challenges. There are three ways in which the Constitution and the government can be adapted to the changing needs and conditions of the country—through amendment, interpretation, and custom.

Why was it important for the Constitution to be flexible?

A because Americans like change.

B because the government needed to be able to adapt to new circumstances and challenges

C because old documents are outdated

D none of the above

The correct answer is **B**.

1 Which president set the two-term tradition?

A George Washington

B John Adams

C Thomas Jefferson

D Benjamin Franklin

2 What were the Democratic and Republican Parties called when they were first created?

F Democrats and Federalists

G Federalists and Republicans

H Labor and Whigs

J Whigs and Tories

3 Who belongs to the executive branch of government?

A the president

B the Supreme Court

C the Senate

D the House of Representatives

4 The Voting Rights Act of 1965 banned voting discrimination based on race or color in federal, state, and local elections. The act also made the use of practices such as literacy tests for voters illegal. As a result of the new law, the number of people who were eligible to vote increased. Write what this means in your own words.

_____

_____

_____

_____

_____

SA Ⓐ Ⓑ Ⓒ Ⓓ   2 Ⓕ Ⓖ Ⓗ Ⓙ   4 Open-ended
1 Ⓐ Ⓑ Ⓒ Ⓓ   3 Ⓐ Ⓑ Ⓒ Ⓓ

5 What is the judicial branch of the government responsible for?

F overseeing the military

G interpreting the laws of the country

H creating the laws of the country

J creating foreign policy

6 Who appoints the vice president?

A the Supreme Court

B the Congress

C the president

D the Speaker of the House

7 What are some of the qualifications for voting in the United States?

F You must be a citizen of the United States.

G You must be 18 years of age.

H both F and G

J none of the above

8 What is the electoral college?

A a group of representatives that determines how colleges should be run

B a group of representatives that votes in the presidential election

C a group of representatives that determines who should be admitted into college

D all of the above

9 Who is the commander in chief?

F the attorney general

G the vice president

H the Speaker of the House

J the president

The map below indicates the number of electoral votes each state had in a recent presidential election. Study the map to answer question 10.

10 Based on what you have learned about electoral votes, which three states were the most heavily populated? How do you know this?

_____

_____

_____

_____

_____

_____

_____

_____

11 Independent candidates usually receive only grassroots support. What does the word grassroots mean?

A the support of poor citizens

B the support of undecided citizens

C the support of the media

D the support from many individuals at the local level rather than from national parties and other large organizations

5 Ⓕ Ⓖ Ⓗ Ⓙ   7 Ⓕ Ⓖ Ⓗ Ⓙ   9 Ⓕ Ⓖ Ⓗ Ⓙ   11 Ⓐ Ⓑ Ⓒ Ⓓ
6 Ⓐ Ⓑ Ⓒ Ⓓ   8 Ⓐ Ⓑ Ⓒ Ⓓ   10 Open-ended

12 Describe a two-party system in your own words.

_____

_____

_____

_____

_____

13 Why was the Declaration of Independence written?

   F to declare the separation of church and state

   G to declare the union of the United States and Great Britain

   H to declare that Great Britain was unfair

   J to declare the United States's independence from Great Britain

14 Where is the Bill of Rights?

   A in the Constitution

   B in the Declaration of Independence

   C in the Mayflower Compact

   D none of the above

15 Who nominates Supreme Court justices?

   F the vice president

   G the president

   H the Speaker of the House

   J all of the above

16 Describe the difference between a <u>primary</u> and a <u>general</u> election.

_____

_____

_____

17 What famous Supreme Court case ended segregation in public schools?

   F *Roe* v. *Wade*

   G *Brown* v. *Board of Education of Topeka*

   H *Porter* v. *Nussle*

   J *Seling* v. *Young*

Study the pie chart showing the percentage of immigrants to the United States in 1820 from Ireland, Britain, Germany, and other places. Then answer questions 18 and 19.

Immigrants to the United States in 1820
Total number of immigrants: 8,385
Places of origin:

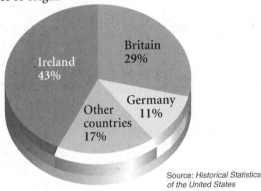

Source: *Historical Statistics of the United States*

18 According to the chart, approximately how many German immigrants came to the United States in 1820?

   F 500

   G 900

   H 1,200

   J 2,500

19 From which country did the most immigrants to the United States come in 1820?

   A Britain

   B Germany

   C Ireland

   D other countries

12 Open-ended   **14** Ⓐ Ⓑ Ⓒ Ⓓ   **16** Open-ended   **18** Ⓕ Ⓖ Ⓗ Ⓙ
13 Ⓕ Ⓖ Ⓗ Ⓙ   **15** Ⓕ Ⓖ Ⓗ Ⓙ   **17** Ⓕ Ⓖ Ⓗ Ⓙ   **19** Ⓐ Ⓑ Ⓒ Ⓓ

71

20 **What does the government spend tax money on?**

    F public education

    G the military

    H roads

    J all of the above

21 **What is an ambassador?**

    A a prince

    B a governor

    C a representative of one country to another country

    D a senator

22 **What is a trade embargo?**

    F restrictions on trade with other countries

    G restrictions on production of goods

    H restrictions on big businesses

    J restrictions on factories

23 **How does the United States determine federal tax rates?**

    A according to income

    B according to age

    C according to level of education

    D according to hours worked

24 **Describe the purpose of the Supreme Court in your own words.**

_____

_____

_____

_____

_____

_____

_____

_____

_____

25 **What is the national debt?**

    F the debt incurred by the citizens of the United States

    G the debt incurred by the businesses of the United States

    H the debt incurred by the government of the United States

    J the debt incurred by the banks of the United States

26 **Which president wrote and delivered the Gettysburg Address?**

    A George Washington

    B Thomas Jefferson

    C Abraham Lincoln

    D John Quincy Adams

20 Ⓕ Ⓖ Ⓗ Ⓙ   **22** Ⓕ Ⓖ Ⓗ Ⓙ   **24** Open-ended   **26** Ⓐ Ⓑ Ⓒ Ⓓ

21 Ⓐ Ⓑ Ⓒ Ⓓ   **23** Ⓐ Ⓑ Ⓒ Ⓓ   **25** Ⓕ Ⓖ Ⓗ Ⓙ

27 Describe the difference between a trade surplus and a trade deficit.

_____

_____

_____

_____

_____

_____

_____

28 What is a monopoly?

   F an autocratic government

   G a situation in which one company controls all production of a good or service

   H a corporation

   J a small business

29 Why are monopolies dangerous to a free-market economy?

   A because they end competition

   B because they may bankrupt small businesses

   C because they control the market

   D all of the above

30 What do interest groups do?

   F promote positive legislation for a particular group of people

   G discourage positive legislation for a particular group of people

   H promote unfair legislation for a particular group of people

   J promote justice for all people

31 Describe the role of a lobbyist.

_____

_____

_____

_____

_____

_____

_____

Study the bar chart about women in the labor force between 1890 and 1930, and then answer question 32.

32 Which of the following statements correctly describes what the bar graph is showing?

   A Most of the women who worked during this period were married.

   B Most of the women who worked during this period were single.

   C Most of the married women during this period did not work.

   D both B and C are correct

Female Labor Force, 1890–1930

Single | Married | Widowed/Divorced

Source: *Historical Statistics of the United States*

Practice Test 5: Listening

Sample A

A   a group of

B   made up of

C   not made up of

D   none of the above

For questions 1–13, darken the circle for the word(s) that best complete the sentence you hear.

1   A   property used to guarantee a loan will be repaid

     B   a signature

     C   a promise by the borrower

     D   a note

2   F   crucial

     G   inconsequential

     H   not necessary

     J   unimportant

3   A   discourage

     B   encourage

     C   prevent

     D   none of the above

4   F   equal power

     G   equality

     H   difference

     J   unequal power

5   A   lack of interest

     B   deep interest

     C   concern

     D   fear

6   F   an economic boom

     G   a severe economic slowdown

     H   an economically prosperous time

     J   a time when the economy is stable

7   A   require a person to come to court

     B   declare a person's innocence

     C   declare a person's guilt

     D   declare the jail time a person is convicted of

8   F   an official decision

     G   an unofficial decision

     H   previous example (see changes on Teacher #8)

     J   none of the above

9   A   kind speech and writing

     B   angry speech and writing

     C   poor speech and writing

     D   fine speech and writing

10   F   excused from

     G   not excused from

     H   made an example of

     J   all of the above

1 Ⓐ Ⓑ Ⓒ Ⓓ   3 Ⓐ Ⓑ Ⓒ Ⓓ   5 Ⓐ Ⓑ Ⓒ Ⓓ   7 Ⓐ Ⓑ Ⓒ Ⓓ   9 Ⓐ Ⓑ Ⓒ Ⓓ
2 Ⓕ Ⓖ Ⓗ Ⓙ   4 Ⓕ Ⓖ Ⓗ Ⓙ   6 Ⓕ Ⓖ Ⓗ Ⓙ   8 Ⓕ Ⓖ Ⓗ Ⓙ   10 Ⓕ Ⓖ Ⓗ Ⓙ

11
  A meager
  B excessive
  C not enough
  D too little

12
  F said
  G lied
  H suggested
  J denied

13
  A feared
  B dispersed
  C came together
  D agreed

Sample B

A occupation
B level of income
C level of education
D level of success

For questions 14–23, listen to the selection your teacher reads. Then darken the circle for the word(s) that best answer the question.

14
  F paralysis
  G polio
  H stroke
  J muscular dystrophy

15
  A because her parents did not believe in public education
  B because she was embarrassed to attend school because of her handicap
  C because the school was not equipped for a handicapped student
  D because she needed one-on-one instruction

16
  F She had to sue the state.
  G She had to graduate cum laude.
  H She had to prove that she was capable of teaching.
  J She had to provide references for her work.

17
  A It educates disabled children in their own homes.
  B It integrates disabled individuals into the community.
  C It provides services for public schools.
  D It educates the public about disabled children.

18
  F George W. Bush
  G Ronald Reagan
  H Bill Clinton
  J Lyndon Johnson

19
  A Disabled in Action
  B Disabled American Veterans
  C the Special Olympics
  D Mothers Against Drunk Driving

20
  F Department of Justice
  G Department of Labor
  H Department of Education
  J Department of the Treasury

21
  A job opportunities for disabled Americans
  B access to public facilities for disabled Americans
  C school conditions for disabled children
  D insurance issues for parents of disabled children

22
  F that one person in this country can make a difference in the lives of other citizens.
  G that all American citizens should be treated equally
  H that positive change is possible if people get involved in the struggle.
  J all of the above

11 (A) (B) (C) (D)   14 (F) (G) (H) (J)   17 (A) (B) (C) (D)   19 (A) (B) (C) (D)   21 (A) (B) (C) (D)   **75**
12 (F) (G) (H) (J)   15 (A) (B) (C) (D)   18 (F) (G) (H) (J)   20 (F) (G) (H) (J)   22 (F) (G) (H) (J)
13 (A) (B) (C) (D)   16 (F) (G) (H) (J)

Teacher's Pages for Listening Test

Listening Passages for Practice Test 5 (pages 74–75)

Directions: For questions 1–13, read each sentence and the four answers aloud. Students should listen carefully to the question and darken the circle for the correct answer.

Sample A

Some interest groups <u>consist</u> of people whose concerns are issue-oriented. <u>Consist</u> means—

A   a group of

B   made up of

C   not made up of

D   none of the above

---

1   Banks require <u>collateral</u> to lend people money. What is <u>collateral</u>?

   A   property used to guarantee a loan will be repaid

   B   a signature

   C   a promise by the borrower

   D   a note

2   An educated public is <u>vital</u> to the preservation of a democratic government. What does the word <u>vital</u> mean?

   F   crucial

   G   inconsequential

   H   not necessary

   J   unimportant

3   Sometimes lobbyists <u>urge</u> local groups and individuals to send letters and telegrams to public officials. What does the word <u>urge</u> mean in this sentence?

   A   discourage

   B   encourage

   C   prevent

   D   none of the above

4   Despite the suggested <u>imbalance</u>, interest groups play an important role in the political process. <u>Imbalance</u> means—

   F   equal power

   G   equality

   H   difference

   J   unequal power

5   The American public's <u>apathy</u> about campaign finance reform only encourages corruption in politics. What is <u>apathy</u>?

   A   lack of interest

   B   deep interest

   C   concern

   D   fear

6 Production, spending, and consumer demand decline during periods of recession. What is a recession?

F an economic boom

G a severe economic slowdown

H an economically prosperous time

J a time when the economy is stable

7 U.S. marshals arrest persons accused of breaking federal laws and also deliver subpoenas. Subpoenas are official documents that—

A require a person to come to court

B declare a person's innocence

C declare a person's guilt

D declare the jail time a person is convicted of

8 George Washington's precedent of a two-term limit has prevented the office of president from gaining too much control. What does precedent mean?

F an official decision

G an unofficial decision

H previous example

J none of the above

9 Dr. Martin Luther King Jr.'s eloquence helped the civil rights movement gain support and approval from white leaders. What does the word eloquence mean?

A kind speech and writing

B angry speech and writing

C poor speech and writing

D fine speech and writing

10 Some organizations are exempt from paying taxes because they are nonprofits. What does the word exempt mean?

F excused from

G not excused from

H made an example of

J all of the above

11 The politician's profuse apology about the misuse of pubic funds did not prevent a hearing in the Senate. What does the word profuse mean?

A meager

B excessive

C not enough

D too little

12 Benjamin Franklin implied that foreign policy was an essential part of American politics? What does the word implied mean?

F said

G lied

H suggested

J denied

13 After September 11, 2001, American citizens rallied to support the World Trade Center victims and their families. What does the word rallied mean?

A feared

B dispersed

C came together

D agreed

Directions: For questions 14–22, the teacher will read the passage and the questions pertaining to the passage aloud. Students should listen carefully to the passage and questions and take notes on a separate sheet of paper. Then, students should darken the circle for the correct answer.

Sample B

Although many citizens throughout our history fought for the right to vote, not everyone exercises this freedom. Voting behavior has attracted the attention of sociologists who have attempted to gauge the importance of education, income, and occupation on voting habits. Studies have revealed that education has the greatest influence on a person's decision to vote. The higher the level of education, the more likely a person is to vote.

Which of the following most influences whether a person votes?

A   occupation

B   level of income

C   level of education

D   level of success

Judy Heumann was born in New York City, where she contracted polio when she was one and a half years old. The illness left her confined to a wheelchair. Because public schools were not equipped to deal with disabled students, she was home-schooled until the fourth grade. After graduation, Heumann studied to become a school teacher. However, the state of New York would not certify her as a teacher due to her physical disability. Heumann won a lawsuit against the state and later helped found Disabled in Action, a disabled-rights organization. She also served with the Centre for Independent Living, which helps integrate disabled individuals into their local communities. Heumann went on to become Assistant Secretary of the Office of Special Education and Rehabilitative Services in the U.S. Department of

Education during the Clinton administration. In this office she worked on improving school conditions for disabled children. Today she works as a consultant on disabled rights and education issues.

14   What disease did Judy Heumann contract as a baby?

F   paralysis

G   polio

H   stroke

J   muscular dystrophy

15   Why was Judy Heumann home-schooled?

A   because her parents did not believe in public education

B   because she was embarrassed to attend school because of her handicap

C   because the school was not equipped for a handicapped student

D   because she needed one-on-one instruction

16   What did Judy Heumann have to do to get a teaching job in the state of New York?

F   She had to sue the state.

G   She had to graduate cum laude.

H   She had to prove that she was capable of teaching.

J   She had to provide references for her work.

17 What service does the Centre for Independent Living provide?

A It educates disabled children in their own homes.

B It integrates disabled individuals into the community.

C It provides services for public schools.

D It educates the public about disabled children.

18 Under what presidential administration did Judy Heumann work?

F George W. Bush

G Ronald Reagan

H Bill Clinton

J Lyndon Johnson

19 Which of the following organizations did Judy Heumann help found?

A Disabled in Action

B Disabled American Veterans

C the Special Olympics

D Mothers Against Drunk Driving

20 Under what U.S. Department does the Office of Special Education and Rehabilitative Services operate?

F Department of Justice

G Department of Labor

H Department of Education

J Department of the Treasury

21 In her job at the Office of Special Education and Rehabilitative Services, what did Judy Heumann work to improve?

A job opportunities for disabled Americans

B access to public facilities for disabled Americans

C school conditions for disabled children

D insurance issues for parents of disabled children

22 What can all Americans learn from the example that Judy Heumann set?

F that one person in this country can make a big difference in the lives of other citizens.

G that all American citizens should be treated equally

H that positive change is possible if people get involved in the struggle

J all of the above

Answer Sheet for Practice Tests

STUDENT'S NAME

LAST	FIRST	MI

SCHOOL:

TEACHER:

FEMALE ○   MALE ○

BIRTH DATE

MONTH	DAY		YEAR	
Jan ○	⓪	⓪	⓪	⓪
Feb ○	①	①	①	①
Mar ○	②	②	②	②
Apr ○	③	③	③	③
May ○		④	④	④
Jun ○		⑤	⑤	⑤
Jul ○		⑥	⑥	⑥
Aug ○		⑦	⑦	⑦
Sep ○		⑧	⑧	⑧
Oct ○		⑨	⑨	⑨
Nov ○				
Dec ○				

GRADE ④ ⑤ ⑥ ⑦ ⑧

(Name grid columns with bubbles A–Z for each letter position)

Fill in the circle for each multiple-choice answer. Write the answers to the open-ended questions in the space provided.

TEST 1   Reading Comprehension

SA Ⓐ Ⓑ Ⓒ Ⓓ   7 Open-ended   14 Ⓐ Ⓑ Ⓒ Ⓓ   21 Ⓕ Ⓖ Ⓗ Ⓙ   28 Ⓐ Ⓑ Ⓒ Ⓓ   35 Ⓕ Ⓖ Ⓗ Ⓙ

1 Ⓐ Ⓑ Ⓒ Ⓓ   8 Open-ended   15 Ⓕ Ⓖ Ⓗ Ⓙ   22 Ⓐ Ⓑ Ⓒ Ⓓ   29 Ⓕ Ⓖ Ⓗ Ⓙ   36 Open-ended

2 Ⓕ Ⓖ Ⓗ Ⓙ   9 Ⓐ Ⓑ Ⓒ Ⓓ   16 Open-ended   23 Open-ended   30 Ⓐ Ⓑ Ⓒ Ⓓ

3 Ⓐ Ⓑ Ⓒ Ⓓ   10 Ⓕ Ⓖ Ⓗ Ⓙ   17 Ⓐ Ⓑ Ⓒ Ⓓ   24 Ⓕ Ⓖ Ⓗ Ⓙ   31 Ⓕ Ⓖ Ⓗ Ⓙ

4 Ⓕ Ⓖ Ⓗ Ⓙ   11 Open-ended   18 Open-ended   25 Open-ended   32 Ⓐ Ⓑ Ⓒ Ⓓ

5 Ⓐ Ⓑ Ⓒ Ⓓ   12 Ⓐ Ⓑ Ⓒ Ⓓ   19 Ⓕ Ⓖ Ⓗ Ⓙ   26 Ⓐ Ⓑ Ⓒ Ⓓ   33 Ⓕ Ⓖ Ⓗ Ⓙ

6 Ⓕ Ⓖ Ⓗ Ⓙ   13 Ⓕ Ⓖ Ⓗ Ⓙ   20 Ⓐ Ⓑ Ⓒ Ⓓ   27 Ⓕ Ⓖ Ⓗ Ⓙ   34 Ⓐ Ⓑ Ⓒ Ⓓ

TEST 2   Reading Vocabulary

SA Ⓐ Ⓑ Ⓒ Ⓓ   2 Ⓕ Ⓖ Ⓗ Ⓙ   4 Ⓕ Ⓖ Ⓗ Ⓙ   6 Ⓐ Ⓑ Ⓒ Ⓓ   8 Ⓐ Ⓑ Ⓒ Ⓓ   10 Ⓕ Ⓖ Ⓗ Ⓙ

1 Ⓐ Ⓑ Ⓒ Ⓓ   3 Ⓐ Ⓑ Ⓒ Ⓓ   5 Open-ended   7 Ⓕ Ⓖ Ⓗ Ⓙ   9 Open-ended

TEST 3 — Language

SA (A) (B) (C) (D)
1 Open-ended
2 (A) (B) (C) (D)
3 (F) (G) (H) (J)
4 (A) (B) (C) (D)

5 (F) (G) (H) (J)
6 (A) (B) (C) (D)
7 (F) (G) (H) (J)
8 Open-ended
9 Open-ended

10 Open-ended
11 (A) (B) (C) (D)
12 (F) (G) (H) (J)
13 (A) (B) (C) (D)
14 Open-ended

15 (F) (G) (H) (J)
16 (A) (B) (C) (D)
17 Open-ended
18 (F) (G) (H) (J)
19 (A) (B) (C) (D)

20 (F) (G) (H) (J)
21 (A) (B) (C) (D)
22 (F) (G) (H) (J)
23 (A) (B) (C) (D)
24 (F) (G) (H) (J)

25 (A) (B) (C) (D)
26 (F) (G) (H) (J)
27 (A) (B) (C) (D)
28 (F) (G) (H) (J)

TEST 4 — Social Science

SA (A) (B) (C) (D)
1 (A) (B) (C) (D)
2 (F) (G) (H) (J)
3 (A) (B) (C) (D)
4 (F) (G) (H) (J)
5 (A) (B) (C) (D)

6 (F) (G) (H) (J)
7 (A) (B) (C) (D)
8 Open-ended
9 (F) (G) (H) (J)
10 (A) (B) (C) (D)
11 (F) (G) (H) (J)

12 (A) (B) (C) (D)
13 (F) (G) (H) (J)
14 (A) (B) (C) (D)
15 (F) (G) (H) (J)
16 (A) (B) (C) (D)
17 (F) (G) (H) (J)

18 (A) (B) (C) (D)
19 (F) (G) (H) (J)
20 Open-ended
21 Open-ended
22 (A) (B) (C) (D)
23 (F) (G) (H) (J)

24 (A) (B) (C) (D)
25 (F) (G) (H) (J)
26 (A) (B) (C) (D)
27 (F) (G) (H) (J)
28 (A) (B) (C) (D)
29 (F) (G) (H) (J)

30 (A) (B) (C) (D)
31 Open-ended
32 (F) (G) (H) (J)

TEST 5 — Listening

SA (A) (B) (C) (D)
1 (A) (B) (C) (D)
2 (F) (G) (H) (J)
3 (A) (B) (C) (D)
4 (F) (G) (H) (J)
5 (A) (B) (C) (D)

6 (F) (G) (H) (J)
7 (A) (B) (C) (D)
8 (F) (G) (H) (J)
9 (A) (B) (C) (D)
10 (F) (G) (H) (J)
11 (A) (B) (C) (D)

12 (F) (G) (H) (J)
13 (A) (B) (C) (D)
14 (F) (G) (H) (J)
15 (A) (B) (C) (D)
16 (F) (G) (H) (J)

SB (A) (B) (C) (D)
17 (A) (B) (C) (D)
18 (F) (G) (H) (J)
19 (A) (B) (C) (D)
20 (F) (G) (H) (J)
21 (A) (B) (C) (D)

22 (F) (G) (H) (J)
23 (A) (B) (C) (D)
24 (F) (G) (H) (J)
25 (A) (B) (C) (D)
26 (F) (G) (H) (J)